The Best
of Branding

The Best of Branding

**Best Practices in
Corporate Branding**

James R. Gregory

McGraw-Hill

New York   Chicago   San Francisco   Lisbon   London
Madrid   Mexico City   Milan   New Delhi   San Juan
Seoul   Singapore   Sydney   Toronto

1 2 3 4 5 6 7 8 9 10 DOC/DOC 0 9 8 7 6 5 4 3

ISBN 0-07-140329-9

Product or brand names used in this book may be trade names or trademarks. Where we believe that there may be proprietary claims to such trade names or trademarks, the name has been used with an initial capital or it has been capitalized in the style used by the name claimant. Regardless of the capitalization used, all such names have been used in an editorial manner without any intent to convey endorsement of or other affiliation with the name claimant. Neither the author nor the publisher intends to express any judgment as to the validity or legal status of any such proprietary claims.

McGraw-Hill books are available at special quantity discounts to use as premiums and sales promotions, or for use in corporate training programs. For more information, please write to the Director of Special Sales, Professional Publishing, McGraw-Hill, Two Penn Plaza, New York, NY 10121-2298. Or contact your local bookstore.

This book is printed on recycled, acid-free paper containing a minimum of 50% recycled, de-inked fiber.

Library of Congress Cataloging-in-Publication Data

Gregory, James R.
  The best of branding : best practices in corporate branding / by James
R. Gregory.
      p.   cm.
Includes index.
  ISBN 0-07-140329-9 (alk. paper)
  1. Brand name products—Management—Case Studies.   2. Brand name products—
Marketing.   I Title.
  HD69.B7.G738 2003
  658.8'27—dc22
                                2003014819

Becky Gregory
and
Bill Gregory

**Our two wonderful children who are always
a source of inspiration**

| Contents

| Acknowledgments

I would especially like to thank Johanna Skilling, who seamlessly translated my thoughts onto the page; she helped make the book that rare combination of business intelligence and a good read.

Special thanks also go to the following people:

Patty Toogood, who kept the entire project organized and moving forward efficiently every step of the way.

Nicholas Giacopelli, who organized and produced all the charts in the book—not once but several times.

Brad Puckey, who provided the data for the charts and for his tireless efforts in maintaining our Corporate Branding Index database.

Stefanie Kubanka, who set up the meetings for the case studies and was involved in managing many of the complexities of such an undertaking.

Barbara Robinson, who energized the project from the start.

For my partners, Larry McNaughton, Karl Barnhart, Andrew Bogucki, Stephen Hooper, and Tim Robinson, who understand and nurture our mutual passion for the subject of corporate branding.

For our clients who make all of this work possible.

And finally to Mary Glenn, our editor at McGraw-Hill, who kept us focused and humored our questions.

| Preface

A WORD ABOUT COREBRAND

CoreBrand is the only branding firm that ties the corporate brand to bottom-line financial and stock performance. We view corporate branding as a disciplined business process, which, when properly thought through and managed, yields tremendous—and tangible—results.

Corporate branding does not come naturally. We believe that the most powerful and successful corporate brands grow out of superior strategies, driven by superior insights, which are then communicated effectively and imaginatively throughout the organization and to the public.

We've studied thousands of organizations, and although no two are exactly alike, we've developed a set of principles that apply to the branding issues faced by every corporation. Our process integrates four fundamental practices, represented by the four divisions within our company:

CoreBrand Intelligence is how we come to understand the brand fundamentals. We integrate standard first-hand and secondary research with our proprietary database to clearly understand how the company rates in the minds and wallets of its key audiences: its strengths, weaknesses, and opportunities for the future. We track each company's return on investment (ROI) on a continuing basis to allow for course corrections and maximizing opportunities for the greatest possible financial returns.

CoreBrand Strategy is how we define the brand essence, the standard behind which the entire company can rally. It is what the company stands for, stated in a way that is relevant to all stakeholders: employees, investors, customers, and others affected by the brand in any way.

CoreBrand Communications creates brand expressions: the words, pictures, icons, and design that represent the brand and create a meaningful image in the minds of the stakeholders.

CoreBrand Management helps our clients build their own brand infrastructure and stay on course over an extended period of time. This is absolutely critical. We know that brands take a long time to build; an educated team within the company can maintain the vigilance required to uphold and grow the brand in the direction defined by *CoreBrand Strategy*.

We've also developed a number of unique tools that show how corporate brands compare to their peers in terms of the strength of their brand, a concept we call CoreBrand Power. Since 1990, with the creation of our Corporate Branding Index, we've developed a comprehensive database of the premier corporate brands, tracking how well—or poorly—they've done business relative to their competitors.

We bring this learning to bear for all of our clients, large and small, through a rigorous process that we call our CoreBrand Analysis. We help senior-level executives understand the value that their brand delivers, how to identify key business opportunities related to the brand, and, just as importantly, how to bring the brand to life and manage its growth.

We're going to share with you just how incredibly powerful the corporate brand can be, and what an overlooked asset it is for the company—perhaps your company.

| Introduction

I have a very special relationship with Apple.

I only use Macintosh computers. But often, when I give speeches in cities around the world, my Mac is not compatible with my hosts' presentation projectors. So in addition to bringing my computer when I travel, I take along my own InFocus projector, and I carry both machines—through airports, hotels, and conference rooms—around the world.

That's how much I love Apple. I'm willing to go through all that effort, and spend a lot more money, because I love interacting with their machines. That's brand value—real value created by Apple Computers.

But does Apple know how much this value is worth—in terms of revenue, stock premiums, or even their market valuation?

Welcome to the Branding Revolution.

For decades, company owners and senior managers have wondered how to measure the value of their brands, and the return on investment for the millions that they spend on corporate communications. The Branding Revolution is all about helping companies create and measure the value of their corporate brands.

It started with a simple question from a CEO who, like many of his peers, wanted to know the ROI from his company's brand communications. It was the person charged with answering this question, GE's Richard Costello, who asked me if we could solve this age-old dilemma. What happened as a result of that conversation changed the dialogue between communicators and senior-level executives forever; it started a true revolution in branding that even now, more than a decade after it started, continues to reverberate around the world.

The analysts and managers at our company share a burning curiosity with me about the causes and effects of branding. Still, we didn't think that finding the connection between brand communications and return on investment was going to be easy, and we were right.

As things turned out, we did not solve the ROI puzzle right away, but we discovered much more than we imagined. We have done a tremendous amount of work to understand precisely how communications affect the brand and the resulting impact on financial performance. Even today, we continue to develop more findings that lead to further research. The journey continues to be fascinating every step of the way.

The key to unlocking the connection between corporate communications and ROI is a concept we call CoreBrand Power. As we'll discuss in detail in Part One, CoreBrand Power is the sum of a company's familiarity and favorability . . . and the way to determine the financial impact of corporate communications on the bottom line.

In order to measure and support our findings on an ongoing basis, we developed a database of over 1000 companies (mostly U.S.-based) across 40 industries, which we call the Corporate Branding Index. We track each of the companies in the Corporate Branding Index according to their reputations, communications, and financial performance. All of our knowledge comes from the long-term study we have conducted from that day to this with our unique database.

The Corporate Branding Index has given us unique insights into the best practices in corporate branding among leading companies from many different industries. We've come to understand which of their actions created more favorable impressions among consumers, financial analysts, and investors. We've seen how outside influences can affect the brand, and what strong brands have done to recover their reputations after a crisis. And we've learned how brands have a direct and measurable result on the bottom line, in terms of improved stock price and market valuation.

This is the first time that we are publicly sharing our findings about the value of corporate brands, along with new case studies from the business community. In the course of reading this book, you'll learn about our insights, based on 30 years of doing business and 13 years of tracking the world's biggest brands. You'll learn about the key steps and best practices required to build a brand and to maximize the ROI from corporate communications of every kind.

The central concept of our work, and this book, is that the brand is a business asset, which can—and should—be managed over time in the same manner as any other business asset. In Part One, you'll find out how we define a brand, how communications can help or hurt, and—most exciting—how much brands contribute to a company's financial performance.

Brands are built over time. When brands are managed on a short-term basis, they make inefficient use of funding, and the results are almost always unimpressive. Usually this turns into a self-fulfilling prophecy: Not enough is spent to have a major impact, and then budgets are slashed because the effort was "not effective." Then, of course, what little impact was created is lost, and there is no opportunity to correct the course and grow the brand.

We challenge the reader to think about branding as a process. In Part Two, you'll read about our four-step process for brand development and management. This process emphasizes the importance of a comprehensive assessment of the company, its customers, and competitors; creating a defined brand and communicating the brand message clearly to all audience segments; managing the brand over time and distance; and measuring results in a consistent and comprehensive way.

This last point raises a big issue. Many companies think they benchmark their performance. Few actually do. At the end of Part

Two, you'll read about the tools we use to track and benchmark, and what most companies do wrong in these areas.

Part Three highlights the case studies we've developed especially for this book. They illustrate the most valuable branding lessons we've identified from our experiences around the world and over the years. We look at each of these companies from a full 360-degree perspective—strategically, from their corporate vision and business objectives; creatively, from their advertising and other communications; and analytically, from the data in our Corporate Branding Index.

Senior managers at each of the companies we've profiled were kind enough to spend a significant amount of time with me to discuss their company's philosophy of branding, internal branding strategies, and specific events in the company's history that affected its Core-Brand Power rating over the past decade.

Examining the information in our database, we analyze the success or failure of these strategies. You'll see how each company fared in terms of its reputation, perception of management, and investment potential, and how each of these attributes were affected—positively or negatively—over time.

We also look at the companies' corporate communications—advertising, employee education, investor relations—examining the planned strategies and tactics employed, and how they affected each company's CoreBrand Power. This is a comprehensive examination of accountability, not a subjective opinion of words and pictures.

There is a universal need among communicators to understand the value of corporate branding and the best practices that will result in improved perception, improved performance, and improved financial results.

This book is our contribution to making the Branding Revolution a reality for your company. We hope it inspires you to help make your corporate brand the best it can be.

Jim Gregory
Stamford, CT

PART ONE
Corporate Brands and the Bottom Line

Chapter One | How Corporate Brands Add Value

WHAT IS A CORPORATE BRAND?

A corporate brand is not a by-product.

It is not an ad campaign, a logo, a spokesperson, or a slogan. Rather, a corporate brand is the product of the millions of experiences a company creates—with employees, vendors, investors, reporters, communities, and customers—and the emotional feelings these groups develop as a result.

Most importantly, a corporate brand is a business asset, one that can return great results to your company when thoughtfully managed over time.

A strong corporate brand delivers a number of outstanding benefits. It commands a premium price. It helps you withstand or weather a crisis more readily. It makes marketing more efficient. It can slow or stop market share erosion. It makes it easier to recruit talent. And it increases your company's appeal to financial and investor markets.

A strong corporate brand creates, manages, and fulfills high expectations among its many audiences. It does this by aligning the fundamentals of the business—products, service, processes, and culture—and giving them a common rulebook, a set of guidelines for making decisions. Companies with a strong brand understand that the way a call is answered on the customer service line is just as important as the headline of its multimillion-dollar ad campaign. They understand that employee motivation and rewards are just as important as media and investor relations.

When your brand is working well, there's a wonderful clarity about your company in the minds of your audiences. They understand who you are and what you do, and they want to be a part of it, whether as a consumer, investor, or employee.

But when the brand is dysfunctional, when it's not actively managed, when decisions are made in "silos," you have what we call an "accidental" brand: The good feelings your company creates are not the result of a long-term strategy but of short-term decisions and a measure of luck. If you have an accidental brand, there is no telling where it may go over time . . . and you have no protection against competition, downturns in the market, or outside circumstances.

Brands are built for the long haul. Some of the best-known brands in the United States have been around for a century or more. We also have our share of new powerhouse brands. With enough funding, focused management, and long-term vision, some of these brands too will be with us a hundred years from now.

EVERY CORPORATION HAS A BRAND

A corporation is a complex entity. It produces multiple products, each under its own brand name, which are marketed to highly segmented audiences. A corporation touches the world in myriad ways: from how its products perform to the size of its dividends, from the design of its building to the benefits it offers its employees. A corporation is a producer, employer, taxpayer, neighbor, service provider, and revenue-maker.

As a result, your corporate brand affects a wide range of audience segments, both internal and external. The internal audiences, of course, include employees, directors, shareholders, vendors, and partners. The external audiences include your consumer markets, the media, investors, regulators, and politicians, even the people in the towns or cities where you do business. All of these people will have expectations and experiences, based on their contact with your brand. And the results of those experiences are important to you.

In our highly interconnected society, we have an innate trust of brands and want to do business with brands we like. We eat the foods they produce, strap our children into the cars they make, trust life-saving operations to products created by corporations we believe in. Many of us place our life savings, and plans for a comfortable retire-ment, in the stocks of corporations we trust to return a healthy profit.

Our collective dependence on corporations for the products we use, the services we enjoy—our very way of life—gives them a place in our national and even global consciousness. And when something goes wrong, from the "dot-bombs" to the fall of Enron, the mistakes corporations make fuel our national debates, dinnertime conversa-tions, even late-night talk show jokes.

The fact is, every corporation has a brand, whether they like it or not, whether they realize it or not, whether or not they have an expen-sive ad campaign or a fancy new logo. A corporation has a brand whether it's selling bread, beer, and mayonnaise or oxygen cylinders and industrial chemicals. A corporation has a brand whether it's in the Fortune 500, in the Russell 2000, or simply listed in the local Yel-low Pages.

In a nutshell, your corporate brand is the sum of everything your company says and does.

The only question is, are you in control of your brand?

When you are, your corporate message will be clear, and your business results will be consistent: Your stock price will reflect your corporation's full value, your sales figures will reflect your customer satisfaction, and your employee turnover will reflect your human resources (HR) and corporate communications strategies. When this is the case, we say that you've achieved *corporate clarity*.

When you're not in control of your brand, either wholly or par-tially, the marketplace will let you know fast. You can see it for your-self in companies you follow: For instance, when a company launches a big corporate campaign, but has paid less attention to the quality of its product or service, its reputation often goes downhill quickly.

We all saw that happen with America Online (AOL), for instance, whose initial push for consumer business resulted in big sales, but whose service wasn't able to keep up with the demand they created. Until AOL built greater capacity, the results were dissatisfaction—even anger—from consumers and diminished trust among analysts. When situations like this happen, we say there's *brand discordance*.

You can fix a dysfunctional brand, of course. You just need to know how . . . and why doing so is so important to your bottom line.

THE POWER OF BRANDING

In the absence of other distinguishing factors, branding is what pushes a consumer to purchase a Maytag washer or a vehicle from General Motors. When you are picking an insurance company, whether for your family or your business, you're more likely to write out your premium checks to the provider who's earned your trust—or whom you believe is trustworthy. That is the power of the corporate brand.

Branding equals trust. Consumers—whether for business or personal products—select brands they believe will serve them best, even if that brand is priced at a premium. Look at American Express: Its basic Personal Card is $65, far more expensive than bankcards. Yet American Express has created a culture of service that provides so much perceived brand value that many consumers are willing to pay more for the "privilege" of using the American Express card.

In addition, the success of the Personal Card allows American Express to continue to create new brand extensions—Gold, Platinum, Blue, and Black, among others—that already have an advantage in the minds of consumers before they're launched, because they carry the imprimatur of the American Express brand.

Sometimes brand value is the result of superior engineering, taste, or other distinguishing factor. But attributes like these are never enough: Your competition can eventually offer something just as good. Think about the "soup wars" between Campbell's and Pro-

---

A DOZEN BENEFITS OF A STRONG CORPORATE BRAND

1. Leads to better business results: sales, earnings, and cash flow
2. Leads to better financial performance, for example, stock price, and price to earnings (P/E) ratio
3. Can command a premium price
4. Creates customer loyalty
5. Makes marketing more efficient
6. Creates differentiation between competitors
7. Makes it easier to recruit and retain talent
8. Can withstand and weather crises more readily
9. Slows or stops share erosion
10. Helps minimize company turf battles, since everyone is working on common goals
11. Appeals to financial and investor markets
12. Helps shape the complex decisions of regulators

---

gresso: In a clash between two essentially similar products, each company has two choices. They can discount their prices, lowering sales revenue and creating a potential financial problem . . . or they can strengthen the brand, so that when customers choose a soup, they're choosing food that will make them feel good, from a brand they can feel good about.

A strong brand drives audiences' experiences in an intentional and consistent way. A strong brand continues strengthening itself, with proper management, by creating a renewable resource of loyal shareholders, customers, and employees. When the pieces fall into place, everything works better for everyone . . . and the brand returns increasing levels of value.

Chapter Two | What Is CoreBrand Power?

CoreBrand Power and the Corporate Branding Index

CoreBrand Power is a simple, logical equation with powerful consequences. In its simplest form, it is the sum of familiarity with the brand, plus favorability toward the brand.

We developed the concept of CoreBrand Power to answer a question that has plagued corporate management since the dawn of the advertising age: How can I tell what my return on investment is going to be from my communications spending?

The marketers and researchers and statisticians at CoreBrand worked on this equation as furiously as scientists trying to create cold fusion. And with about as much success. But then came the "eureka" moment. Advertising and communications may not affect return on investment (ROI) directly . . . but CoreBrand Power does.

Every year since 1990, our company has surveyed the CoreBrand Power of 1000 companies in over 40 industries. Our researchers call 10,000 decision makers each year, asking for their opinions on each company's familiarity and favorability. We also track each company's financial performance and communications. As a result, we've accumulated a tremendous amount of data that lets us track brand histories and CoreBrand Power over time. We call this our Corporate Branding Index.

The familiarity rating is based on each respondent's own familiarity with the company, a self-selecting measure based on a five-point scale, from "unfamiliar" to "very well known."

The respondents who have some familiarity with a company then rate favorability on a four-point scale, according to three attributes: Overall Reputation, Perception of Management, and Investment Potential. Together, these three attributes form the favorability score.

> *Familiarity + Favorability =*
> *CoreBrand Power*

Finally, we combine each company's familiarity and favorability scores to establish its CoreBrand Power score on a scale of 0 to 100. We track the scores over time, and against competitive companies, to see both the movement of the company's CoreBrand Power over the previous years, and how well—or poorly—it compares to its peers: See Figure 2-1.

Even a superficial look at CoreBrand Power scores across an industry can show where a company fits in relative to its competitors. Figure 2-2 illustrates the strengths and weaknesses of some of America's leading pharmaceutical brands. As the chart shows,

- *Leading brands* have both high familiarity and high favorability. The challenge is to maintain their favorable positions.
- *Promising brands* score low on familiarity but high on favorability. They have an opportunity to enhance their corporate brands through increased communications.

WHO DO WE TALK TO?

The respondents to our CoreBrand Power survey are senior business executives who are familiar with brands as both B-to-B (Business-to-Business) purchasers and everyday consumers. Each respondent rates a total of 40 companies.

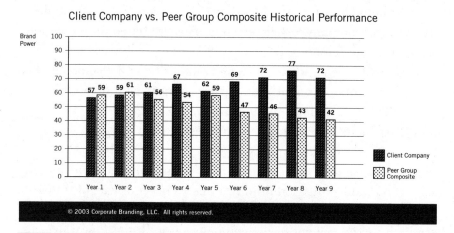

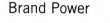

Figure 2-1. Brand power

- *Infamous brands* are those with high familiarity but low favorability. The opportunity here is to "fix what's broke"—and make sure the world finds out about it.
- *Challenged brands* are those with low scores on both familiarity and favorability. The silver lining is that there is nowhere to go but up.

When we drill down into favorability, we can also look at how the various attributes—Overall Reputation, Perception of Management, and Investment Potential—perform over time. There's a normal distribution of the attributes: Reputation is usually rated the highest, with perceptions of management in the middle, and investment potential at the bottom.

When the lines representing the three attributes get closer together, it demonstrates *corporate clarity*. As we discussed in Chapter 1, achieving clarity means that your brand is working, your messages are in sync with one another, and your business results will reflect those synergies. In some extreme cases, clarity can be a double-

A Place on the Map

Our researchers plotted the corporate brands on a familiarity/favorability quadrant to paint a visual picture of their positions relative to each other and to diagnose strategies for increasing their brand power.

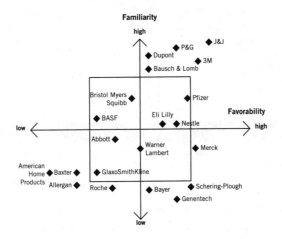

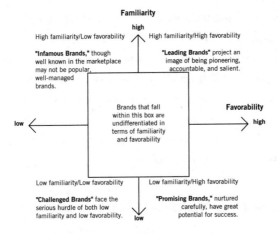

Figure 2-2. A place on the map

Building Clarity and Momentum

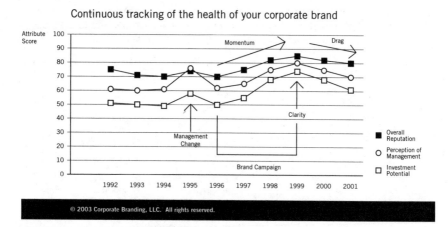

Continuous tracking of the health of your corporate brand

Figure 2-3. Favorability attributes

edged sword: A troubled company can also achieve corporate clarity. In those cases, the lines will be moving together, too . . . but in a downward direction.

When we see the attributes spread, or *drag*, it indicates confusion about the company. This suggests that the brand is not being managed properly, or perhaps that there is a crisis that temporarily shakes the outside world's faith until the company proves it can get back on its feet. Take a look at Figure 2-3 to see what we mean.

Identifying issues that are affecting your company's CoreBrand Power can also help you address them, managing your way back to corporate clarity, and a stronger brand.

HOW COMMUNICATIONS AFFECT THE BRAND

We all know intuitively that corporate brand communications—any corporate, brand, or trade advertising carrying the corporate name— should improve familiarity. The more you advertise, the better your company is known.

When you are in control of your messages, and those messages are strategically sound and aligned with your vision of the brand, greater familiarity also leads to improved favorability: People who know your company are more likely to feel positive toward it than a company they know less well. And often, those positive feelings lead to action: purchasing your product, investing in your stock. Those actions in turn lead to business results: stronger cash flow, higher stock price, even improved market valuation. Figure 2-4 illustrates this process.

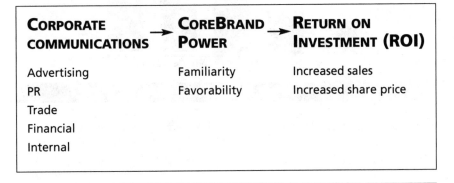

Figure 2-4. The impact of corporate communications on ROI can be quantified by assessing the brand's CoreBrand Power.

In fact, advertising is the single biggest driver of CoreBrand Power, accounting, on average, for about 30 percent of each company's CoreBrand Power score. Other important factors include the size of the company (23 percent), and corporate communications, such as employee relations and investor relations (22 percent).

Looking more deeply at the data, we find some interesting correlations between strong levels of advertising and high levels of Core-Brand Power.

Twenty percent of the companies we reviewed accounted for almost 90 percent of total corporate ad spending. The top 20 percent of companies spent an average of more than $140 million annually, while the lowest 40 percent spent less than a million dollars per year . . . and some spent nothing at all. Figure 2-5 shows how CoreBrand Power is affected by a company's advertising investment.

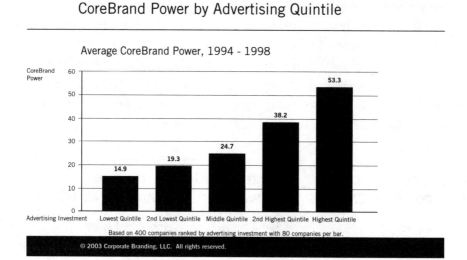

Figure 2-5. CoreBrand Power versus corporate advertising investment

Importantly, the top 20 percent in terms of ad spending were also the top companies in terms of CoreBrand Power, with an average CoreBrand Power score of over 50. The lowest 40 percent of companies had an average CoreBrand Power score of about 17.

Of course, this raises the question: Does your company have to be a Coca-Cola or Microsoft to register on the scale? No . . . but among your company's peer group, the one who invests most effectively in advertising and corporate communications is the one who'll have the edge in CoreBrand Power.

SO IS COREBRAND POWER JUST A FUNCTION OF SPENDING MORE MONEY?

Interestingly enough, we've found that there is a point of diminishing returns when it comes to advertising budgets. Contrary to the advice of many advertising agencies, who would always have their clients spend more, we can tell how much a company needs to spend to achieve maximum CoreBrand Power . . . and at what point each dollar spent becomes less effective.

On the one hand, low levels of advertising, relative to your industry, can be completely ineffective: Your message has to be communicated powerfully enough within your market segments to break through what we call the "threshold of indifference." Once that point is reached, incremental brand advertising will begin to yield increasing returns on CoreBrand Power.

There comes a point, however, when the level of spending becomes less efficient, and your company will begin to get decreasing returns from each dollar spent on advertising. Using this model, which we call the Advertising Efficiency Curve (see Figure 2-6), you can see not only the level of investment that will be most effective for your company but also where you can consider actually capping that investment.

Of course, any corporate brand advertising or corporate communication needs to be strategically sound, or whatever amount you spend will be largely wasted in terms of your CoreBrand Power. We'll get into the process of creating effective strategies in Part 2.

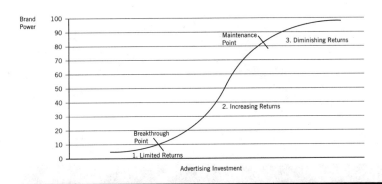

Figure 2-6. Advertising Efficiency Curve

BUT HOW CAN I TELL WHAT MY INVESTMENT IS WORTH?

Let's take this a step further. When you invest in your brand, through advertising and corporate communications, you can see the impact on your company's market valuation.

This is a big breakthrough. Traditionally, and I mean until right this minute, most CEOs and CFOs have tended to look at advertising and other marketing communications as expendable: These budgets are often the first to go when a company gets into a financial crunch. Unfortunately, corporate communications managers have had no ammunition to back up their arguments that more spending might help the brand, rather than hurt it.

Here's that ammunition.

Take a look at Figure 2-7. The straight line represents increasing levels of spending on brand communications; the curved line represents market value. The higher the spending line goes, the more it pushes up

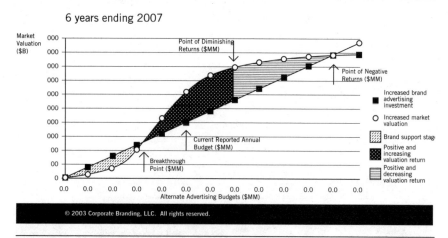

Figure 2-7. Advertising return analysis

Can You Calculate the Actual Dollar Value that CoreBrand Power Adds to Your Market Cap?

The answer is yes.

The first step is to understand what a given company's familiarity and favorability—its CoreBrand Power—would be if it had never invested in its brand. (We know it's higher than zero, because no matter what, there are employees, stockowners, customers, and other people who are familiar with the brand. Companies of a certain size also have a level of built-in familiarity, which in turn leads to increased favorability.)

To do this, we select the companies in our database with the lowest level of CoreBrand Power, and create a baseline for low market valuation by estimating their cash flow multiple, stock price, and market cap.

Then we compare financial statistics for companies of similar size, in similar industries, that have focused on their corporate brand. The result: We can see the amount—often in the millions of dollars—that CoreBrand Power adds to the valuation of well-managed corporations.

---

the market cap . . . until, like the Advertising Efficiency Curve we saw in Figure 2-6, it arrives at a point of diminishing returns.

Using this model for individual companies, we've found that we can *pinpoint the budget* a company needs to allocate to brand communications in order to reach its maximum market valuation at the greatest efficiency. That gives you two clear, definitive options: Take the opportunity to leverage your brand more effectively, or leave a lot of money on the table. Take that to your CFO!

Communications is clearly an important investment for your brand. But communicators—those in the business of public relations, advertising, employee relations, sales, and marketing—often have a terrible inability to communicate the value of their work to senior-level executives, who invariably want to know the impact on the bottom line.

Many, if not most, companies also face the problem of in-house cooperation, or lack of it; this is often the result of different communications groups fighting for a share of a shrinking communications budget. Managers in charge of public relations (PR), investor relations (IR), advertising, sales, and marketing all feel the need to protect their turf from budget cuts—and, if possible, get a bigger share of a limited budget.

Understanding the potential return on investment can help everyone, senior management included, to break out of their silos and work collectively to get the most impact from their corporate brand communications.

Chapter Three | How Corporate Brands Contribute to Financial Performance

HOW COREBRAND POWER AFFECTS YOUR STOCK PRICE

Companies that improve their CoreBrand Power usually improve their financial performance as well. Since 1990, we've seen that brand leaders significantly outperform their competitors in terms of stock price growth. We've also seen that stock price usually increases when a company improves its CoreBrand Power.

As you probably know, there are two basic reasons that stock prices change. Either there's a change in company performance, for example, sales, cash flow, earnings, dividends, and book value, or a change in the multiples (or premiums) that the market grants to a company based on past performance and expected future performance.

There are many factors, both financial and psychological, that affect these multiples. Among them are financial strength, past stock price growth, expected future growth in cash flow and earnings, company size, recent price and earnings trends, earnings as a percentage of cash flow, dividend yield, stock price volatility, and level of price.

The Financial Factor

Many elements affect brand power, which, in turn, affects stock value.

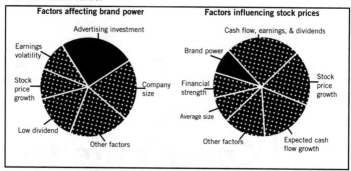

Source: Value Line Investment Survey, Competitive Media Reporting, and Corporate Branding Index annual survey

Figure 3-1. The financial factor

But investors place a higher premium on the cash flow, earnings, and book value of a company with a higher level of CoreBrand Power. Companies with higher levels of CoreBrand Power tend to see, on average, a 5 to 7 percent premium *added to their stock price.* Companies with lower CoreBrand Power are often losing the incremental stock value that a higher level of CoreBrand Power would provide. Figure 3-1 illustrates the point.

EVEN ANALYSTS ARE AFFECTED BY THE BRAND

Every CEO and CFO knows that financial analysts need detailed reports and projections about their corporation. What they may not know is that the job of communicating with this essential audience doesn't stop there.

We went out and asked financial analysts what other kinds of information influence their research and recommendations. Interestingly, a majority of the analysts we spoke to told us that corporate advertising often motivates them to research a company further.

Virtually every one of the analysts we spoke to said that corporate communications are "important" in determining stock value. Fifty percent cited corporate advertising as the most effective way to create a positive image for the company. They also told us that the messages developed specifically for them are more credible if they're consistent with communications delivered to other critical audiences—such as employees, customers, and the media.

But here's the downside—or, put another way, the opportunity. According to our survey, fewer than a third of financial analysts believe that companies consistently communicate who they are and where they are going. That's a lot of potential leverage left on the table—and a lot of communications dollars that could be used more effectively.

CoreBrand Power versus the S&P 500

We wanted to see for ourselves if we could find out how the brand affects stock price. It's not that we thought that CoreBrand Power would be the most important factor in determining stock price. As we said above, earnings, cash flow, dividends, and growth are the primary drivers. But we wondered if an investment approach that included CoreBrand Power could help improve portfolio returns.

We assembled detailed information on hundreds of companies and developed a model, which predicted changes in stock prices over 13 weeks. In addition to CoreBrand Power, taken from our Corporate Branding Index, the model incorporated thousands of pieces of data, including financial factors from The Value Line Investment Survey, Investor's Business Daily, and corporate advertising data from TNS Media Intelligence/CMR.

Based on all of this, we created a hypothetical stock portfolio and placed a hypothetical bet. If we'd used real money it would have been a very big bet: We "invested" $750,000 in a portfolio based on the model we had developed, and placed the same hypothetical amount in the S&P 500. We began our experiment in October 1999.

> ## THE RULES OF THE GAME
>
> To keep things consistent, we developed a set of rules to manage our model portfolio:
>
> - The portfolio is limited to a maximum of 15 stocks, with no more than three additions each week.
> - A set of buy and sell rules was developed so that buy/hold/sell decisions can be made automatically. In periods of market weakness the rules permit reducing the portfolio to fewer than 15 stocks.
> - Trades occur on Monday mornings and are assumed to be at the Friday closing price.
> - To be included in the selection process a company must:
>   - Be publicly traded in the United States
>   - Have an above-average CoreBrand Power rating in the United States
>   - Be included in The Value Line Investment Survey of 1700 companies
> - *The model rules.* A quantitative model predicts the likely intermediate term stock price change of each of the companies at any point in time. A spreadsheet model keeps information current and calculates the ratings of each company on an ongoing basis. Thus, at each weekly update we can rate and rank all companies on the basis of their likely stock price performance over the next 3 months.
> - A separate model forecasts the likely 13-week change in the S&P 500 index. This is based on weekly data for the past 8 years.
> - Our research has shown that the factors driving stock prices are dynamic, and change as market conditions change. Thus the models are adaptive, with changes periodically made to both the model structure and the model parameters.

Between October 1999 and August 2001, the S&P 500 fell about 7 percent. The original hypothetical investment of $750K in the S&P was now worth $696K. By contrast, our model returned about 71 percent during the same period. Our $750K investment, which we now of course wished was real money, was worth $1,284K. [These figures do not include interest on moneys in cash equivalents (when the portfolio has fewer than 15 stocks) or dividends. At a 5 percent per year interest rate, the cash equivalents would have added another $28,500 to the portfolio total. The interest and dividends are assumed to approximately offset transaction costs and management fees.]

It wasn't a straight upward climb. We learned that the role of the brand changes, along with the impact it has on financial performance, as market conditions change. For instance, the brand does not give the same premium to your stock price as other factors when there's a recession going on.

We learned that, in relationship to your financial performance, managing your corporate brand is like driving a car. There are times when you can accelerate spending on corporate communications and image-driven activities and gain more mileage from the brand. There are other times when you can slow down and rely on the momentum of your company's CoreBrand Power to get you over the rough spots.

It's important to note that the corporate brand's role never disappears: It remains the standard which your company upholds. But understanding when the corporate brand's role increases and decreases in relationship to other factors can help you manage your brand—and your stock price—more effectively in changing climates.

PART TWO
Four Steps to a Better Branding Process

Chapter	**Step One:**
Four	**Discovery**

UNDERSTANDING THE BRAND DYNAMICS

Most of the time, there's a trigger event.

Companies decide it's time to examine their brand for any number of different reasons. Larry McNaughton, CoreBrand's Managing Director and Chief Operating Officer (COO), says that "It can be something as grand and glorious as a merger and acquisition; something as inglorious as a failure in a product or an embarrassing business strategy that becomes public.

"It could be something as mundane as the company chairman saying to somebody on his team, 'hey, Dave, what is our brand all about?' " McNaughton continues. "And when Dave begins to answer in a less than satisfying way, more than likely talking about things like advertising, or the corporate identity, or company name, the chairman says, 'that's not what I'm talking about. I'm talking about what people think of us. Does that have any impact on what we do?' "

Thus begins the process of discovering the brand.

When we "discover" a brand, much like prospectors looking for gold, we often discover an asset that is already there: valuable attributes and ideas that exist deep inside the corporation but have not been brought to light. Of course, we also find our share of "fool's gold": attitudes and attributes that hinder the good experiences you want your audiences to have with your company.

So the discovery process is an exploration based on our simple definition of the brand, that is, a corporate asset that is defined, dimensionalized, and described by the sum of experiences that it creates. As the process unfolds, it becomes easier and easier to distinguish the attributes that make your brand uniquely valuable, and determine which aspects of the company aren't in alignment.

The first step in the exploration is to understand which audiences are important to your business, and what each of their experiences has actually been. Understanding the image, reputation, and perceptions that each audience maintains about your corporation helps you learn what you can capitalize on—or correct—in order to organize the brand as an asset.

From the Inside Out

The first stop is the corner office: In the best practices of well-branded companies, the leader's ownership of the brand is vital. A CEO's history with the company tends to have a significant impact on how he or she perceives and therefore manages the brand; it also often influences his or her plans for leading the organization in the near future.

McNaughton explains, "Clearly, you want to know the CEO's own personal experiences as a human being, relative to this brand. Perhaps he started in the mailroom and worked his way up; perhaps she was recruited from a competitor just a year ago."

McNaughton tells us that the process of discovery for company leaders begins with conversations, followed by a review of things that they've done in the recent past.

"That could be as simple as looking at all of the speeches, documents, and calls to action that they've sent out to the troops," McNaughton says. "You can see if there's a common theme, if there are common personas that are expressed. You can also see if there are any contradictions, which happens fairly frequently, in what they say to the rest of the world."

The second step is also an internal exploration: understanding the perspectives and experiences of both the operational management and line employees. Depending on the size and organization of the company, this can be a hugely complex task; as a result, it's important to identify not only all the internal organizations and their chains of command, but to use a combination of qualitative and quantitative research to get the most accurate picture possible.

For instance, McNaughton says, "For operational managers, you might either have personal interviews with them, and view their own materials, or you may do some form of research. It could be as simple as very focused group discussions, or it could be more quantitative.

"We might do a survey, for example, which can be done by phone, posted on the company Web site, or printed and distributed to both the operational managers and the employees up and down the line."

Depending on the breadth, depth, and complexity of your company, this process of discovery and exploration can take anywhere from a few weeks to over a year. Of course, the length of time is a function of the company's willingness to invest, the importance it places on its brand, and the immediate need. Sometimes a corporation has the luxury to do a full exploration of its brand; at other times, there may be a major event, such as a merger or initial public offering (IPO) that will require a faster solution.

No matter how long the process takes, company executives need to be prepared for what they might hear. As McNaughton reveals, "Sometimes objectivity is a little jarring." The executives prepared to accept the results of the discovery process are those who have the greatest opportunity to maximize their brand.

The Outside World

In addition to establishing the internal perspectives on the brand, it's critical to find out what the outside world thinks. As we discussed in Chapter 1, a company's outside audiences are typically far-ranging, including not only customers, investors, and financial analysts but quite often union leaders, regulators, politicians, national and local media, and residents of the towns and cities where your company has operations. Because of the size of those groups, and the various segments within them, quantitative research tends to be more effective—and persuasive—than qualitative, although there's a place for both.

Often, corporations already have huge treasure troves of research that you can mine.

McNaughton observes, "Many companies spend an awful lot of money on research and don't really do very much with it. So they've got rooms full of information on various audiences, including the internal audience, that they've used for one or two numbers that they presented at a board or management meeting. And they're often not aware of exactly what else is in there."

FACTORING IN COREBRAND POWER

The discovery process is also where we first start employing our Core-Brand Analysis to bring an added level of intelligence to the brand's dynamics. For many companies, we can examine a dozen years of data, based on the information in our Corporate Branding Index. As we discussed in Chapter 2, this part of the process allows us to determine several key pieces of information:

- The company's current CoreBrand Power rating
- The movement (up or down) of its rating over the last 12 years
- The driving forces behind that movement (familiarity, favorability)
- The company's financial history in terms of stock price, price to earnings ratio (P/E), and valuation, and how those compare to its CoreBrand Power
- Its place in a competitive mix of similar companies

This information provides an objective framework against which to measure the information we retrieve in the course of exploring the perceptions and inner workings of the company. Often, it becomes very clear that a change in management or business process created a

shift in the public's perception of the company—either up or down;
the data give us a concrete way to show company management the
effects of their actions.

DISTILLATION

Eventually, all of the vast array of experiences from the many audience segments, both internal and external, must be organized in a way
that makes the information relevant and actionable for understanding
the corporate brand. At CoreBrand, we assign all of the information
from the exploration into one of three categories:

- Business processes
- Communications
- Cultures and behaviors

We then create a matrix that allows us to examine each audience's
perspective in each of these three key areas. The areas that are uni-
formly strong may become the cornerstones of the brand's identity.
Conversely, the disconnects that become obvious using this method
reveal opportunities for changing the way your company does business—whether by identifying business processes that aren't working
as well as possible, communications that aren't as effective as they
could be, or ways of relating to employees that could be strengthened.

As McNaughton explains, "You begin to understand the leadership perspective on business processes, for instance, compared to the
experiences of operational employees and current customers. You can
look at the same issue from the perspective of analysts, regulatory
agencies, and unions, or whoever it might be. And you start looking
for the highest common denominators, as well as the disconnects.

"Let me offer you a simple tactical example," McNaughton continues. "Let's say you find out that analysts associate Company X
with a reputation for fraud. That's an experience and a perception
that Company X has somehow created. On the one hand, the leadership in companies are human beings, and they can be hugely defen-
sive. They might simply say, 'We're not fraudulent, we're not thieves,'

and let the matter drop. So although they may be right, that won't solve the problem.

"The enlightened folks say, 'We'd better do something about that.' They see the information as an insight, and look for ways to change that perception."

BRAND ANALYSIS

The discovery process culminates in what we call a CoreBrand Analysis. The CoreBrand Analysis transcends the tactical steps needed to make changes and provides direction for making those changes in a systemic, justifiable, and positive way that builds the brand.

It's complex, but it comes down to a very simple thing—the ability to explain in a simple and clear way what your company is all about, that is both believable and supported by the history and experiences that the company has created.

As an example, McNaughton cites the case of a company that needed to change the perception that it was not a dinosaur in an industry soon to become extinct.

"This is a very large printing company," McNaughton explains. "It's a wonderful company that's been around for 90 years. They make traditional three-part forms printed with ink on paper, the sort of thing you get when you buy a large appliance, or when you register at college. They thought about themselves as a printing company that makes forms, and everything they did was based around that.

"With the advent of technology and the acceptance of technology, and especially the acceptance of a digital document as something that's as real as any other document, they started to wonder if they should be doing something different. In some ways, anybody who's in the information business, a database company for instance, could come in and say, you don't need printed forms anymore, they're obsolete.

"We took a look at the company and realized that, despite the way they marketed themselves, they actually had a big business in digital business information, but we also came to realize that, at least in the foreseeable future, there will always be a need for the printed form.

"So then we asked ourselves, what business are they really in? Are they in the business of creating digital documents? Creating paper and ink documents? Or are they in an entirely different business? After going through the discovery process, taking a look at their business internally, examining their competition, and talking to their customers, we defined them as being in the business of capturing and transforming transactions, instead of simply being a printing company that makes forms.

"So if they begin to think of their brand as 'capturing the transactions,' they can use that to explain every part of their business, from capturing, organizing, and manipulating information, to giving that information back to the business managers. What's more, they can consider almost any decision regarding their business processes, communications, and culture based on that standard."

Chapter Five | Step Two: Strategy

DEFINING THE ESSENCE OF THE BRAND

Once you've completed the discovery process, you know what your brand represents, and to whom. You know which key points about your company are currently understood by key audience segments, and where there are gaps. You've defined what your company stands for, and what you want it to stand for in the foreseeable future.

The next step is to develop a strategy for communicating this vision of the brand.

Tim Robinson, CoreBrand Strategy's Managing Director, says, "The key part of this step is to distill the essence of the brand down to something that can be translated throughout the company: to marketing and communications as well as to your business processes, vendor relations, financial analyst relations, and customer service."

Your strategy expresses your brand personality, and the promise you make to your stakeholders. It is the cornerstone of the expectations you want your stakeholders to have of your company, and the linchpin of everything you want your company to stand for and act on.

As we discussed in Part 1, companies that have strong strategies tend to perform better in the stock market. They tend to retain both employees and customers longer.

Your brand strategy articulates what you want people to experience when they interact with your company. It allows your audiences to understand who you are and why you're doing what you do.

Robinson explains, "That's important, because people want to work for or work with or invest in companies that they understand. If the company is a mystery box, it tends to make people shy away. Presenting your company in a way that fairly represents who you are, and in a way that's attractive to your stakeholders, is key to your success in business."

Just as in the discovery phase, the CEO is a key player in providing input and approval for the brand strategy. In addition, the team needs to include the chief marketing officer, chief financial officer, and other corporate leaders. There may also be a place at the table for operational managers in corporate marketing and communications, as well as brand strategists from individual product lines.

There is, however, no room for individual or unit agendas when formulating a corporate brand strategy. Robinson says that no matter whether the people responsible for creating your brand strategy are executives, employees, or partners coming in from outside, "they need to be part of a team, as somebody who genuinely wants to solve the company's business needs, and be in the process with truly honorable intentions."

UNLOCKING THE BRAND

In the discovery process, you uncovered the positive and negative experiences of the company. In the strategic phase, Robinson explains, "The brand strategy is developed by overlaying the learning from each piece of the discovery process, understanding where the common threads are, and clearly defining who the company is, what they do, and why they are different from anybody else."

As Robinson suggests, differentiation is a key element of a successful strategy. A truly differentiated company is able to charge a premium for its goods or services. The more alike products and companies are—or are perceived to be—the less leverage there is to charge a premium above the raw cost of production.

Many companies simply like to say that they are the "best" in their class of product or service. But that alone is not enough. The claim has to be supportable.

For instance, as Robinson observes, "A more expensive pen like Mont Blanc is clearly differentiated from a basic ballpoint on its features, design, and the feeling of performance. That's why a Mont Blanc will cost you $225 and another type will cost a dollar. Certainly there's a role for the dollar pen, but differentiation allows Mont Blanc to charge a premium for the product they make—and the experience they deliver."

Identifying the differentiating factors of your brand can often create an "aha!" moment.

As Robinson says, "The thing about my job that continues to excite me is the opportunity to pinpoint the idea that drives a company differently from its competitors, and how they can succeed at that."

What's the Difference between Brand Strategy and Advertising?

Brand strategy has a long-term objective; advertising has a relatively short-term objective. There are exceptions. Some companies have taken their advertising and made it their brand or communicated their brand strategy very effectively through advertising, but it's rare.

As Robinson says, "Advertising is the icing on the cake, so to speak. It's the glitter, it's the gloss, it's the thing that will help build awareness, but not the thing that will necessarily help build the brand."

A corporate brand strategy affects virtually every aspect of the company, including advertising, but also such disparate elements as customer service, product delivery, and employee relations.

A TECHNOLOGY COMPANY TAKES A STEP INTO THE FUTURE

The Omron Corporation is a Japanese manufacturer whose primary business lies in making high-tech components for industrial and healthcare products. Despite its 70-year history and 24,000 employees, Omron was largely unknown among many of its potential customers and investors. Omron's senior management realized that in order to grow, they needed to break through that lack of awareness and become known not only as a components manufacturer but also as a technology leader.

One of Omron's core technologies is sensors. The technology of this business was evolving to the point that it could soon help machines take over much of the work that humans do in dirty, possibly dangerous, situations. This advanced technology was a key differentiator in the marketplace and, as a result, suggested the focus of the brand exploration.

Tim Robinson explains, "We did research to understand the history of the organization, the market dynamics, and their business strategy. And we were able to distill a couple of key points that related to foresight, that is, Omron's ability to understand needs that weren't on the table yet, but would be in the very near future.

"So we developed a brand strategy that was based around the idea of 'sensing tomorrow,'" Robinson continues. " 'Sensing' being based in the core technology that they're leveraging for the future, plus the philosophy of creating and adapting products to solve future needs. The brand is 'sensing tomorrow,' and that position explains their business to customers and employees and shareholders."

Robinson explains, "Many companies tend to pigeonhole activities and don't really think as much about implications across the entire corporation. But when we develop a brand strategy, we're not only thinking about communications, but also about the management component, the business processes, the corporate culture."

Tactical solutions of any kind rarely address the brand issues.

Robinson says, "Sometimes, a client thinks that all they need is a new logo, when in fact, their problem is not a logo or a brochure, but how they're positioned versus their competitors. A logo can be a symbol of that change, but isn't always the change that's needed."

Larry McNaughton agrees: "Discussing the difference between creating a brand strategy and creating communications can get a little bit difficult, primarily because leadership and managers don't think of the brand as an asset, but rather, as something to do. Like advertising for the corporate identity, or saying, 'Let's give out T-shirts to the employees,'—and thinking, 'now we're making a brand.'

"But are they?" McNaughton continues. "Yes, they're using things to express the brand, but they haven't described what the brand is. I could give out all the T-shirts in the world and never influence the brand one iota, if I didn't do it very well.

"But if I understand what the brand is," McNaughton says, "that is, the sum of experiences that the company has created, and wants to create in the future—the brand strategy is the summation that will influence the decisions that consumers, or buyers, or employees, or investors will make from here on in."

"The part that I think about a lot," Robinson adds, "is how can this strategy be the touchstone for all activities of the business? How can we factor in future endeavors, future growth, future partnerships, or alliances in relation to this strategy?"

Chapter Six | Step Three: Communications

BRINGING THE BRAND TO LIFE

The brand strategy lends itself to two practical—and inextricable—applications. The first of these is corporate communications.

Tim Robinson explains that the transition from brand strategy to communications is in "understanding the linkages between the market levers that the company has: what it is they bring to the market, the customer opportunity, what exists out there that other companies aren't taking advantage of, and the history and philosophy of the organization. And once we can define those linkages, the creative process is how we best explain them to the different audiences that are important.

"What we try to do when we move from strategy to communications," Robinson continues, "is to end the strategy phase in a way that creates a platform for communications development."

Each situation has unique communications needs. Andrew Bogucki, CoreBrand Communications' Creative Director, says "Companies will come to us in various stages of their development and, depending on where they are, the process will be a little different. They could be a pure startup, or a merger, which is a totally different ball of wax. Or it could simply be an updating, a refreshing, and a refocusing.

"With a startup," Bogucki says, "there's no equity, no history to draw upon or to research. It's about purely taking that strategy and coming up with the best execution.

"But if a company is long established," Bogucki continues, "we do an audit of all the material they've done in the past, and an audit of what their competitors are doing. In a merger, you've got two sets of material to look at. The big thing in those cases is equity. Their brands have been around, they've built equity in something. Maybe it's a color, maybe it's a font; we have to take all that into consideration. But what we try to do is understand what's out there, what we can leverage, and if we can use it appropriately."

In the Beginning

Brand identities are almost never the result of a lone genius creating work behind closed doors. Since the brand needs to ultimately speak to and appeal to a wide variety of constituencies, it only makes sense that a strong brand is the result of a strong collaboration.

Karl Barnhart, CoreBrand Communications' Managing Director, concurs: "You need an identity, visually, verbally, and holistically. Once you've developed your criteria and strategy, you start the brainstorming process to sit down and bring that to life."

Andrew Bogucki agrees, with a twist: "I think the net result is stronger due to the collaborative process. But you don't get there without the strength of individual efforts.

"The fact is, creative expression is a very personal thing," Bogucki continues. "You created it, feel good about it, you even stuck it on the wall. And you can get blind to the potential negatives; that's natural. But that's where the group comes into play and makes it stronger.

"Because nine times out of ten, after the person has huffed off and looked at the stuff that the group told them they should look at again, they come back and say, 'You're right, that's actually better.' So you need the energy from the individuals to create the raw material, and you need the group to help strengthen the good ideas and weed out the not-so-great ideas."

The brainstorming process casts a wide net. As Bogucki describes the process at CoreBrand, "We'll take the design team, and the strategy team, and get them all in a room and say, here is the strategy, including the brand promise and the brand personality.

"We ask ourselves, which aspects of the brand lend themselves to a visual translation?" Bogucki continues. "What can we start articulating? Some of it is either too specific or too esoteric, but there are always other ideas that we can grab onto. We'll just scrawl stuff down and wallpaper the room. Sometimes we try to focus the ideas, sometimes it's hugely broad. It depends on the project, but the process is the same, just the scale shifts. At the end of that, we try to come up with four or five 'buckets' to start designing against. For instance, let's say one aspect of the strategy is strength and stability: What are all the different visual ways that make sense for us to communicate that?

"Then we give people a couple of days to put together some ideas, and we gather again," Bogucki says. "We start talking about what's up there, what's working, what isn't, what do we respond to. The challenge is to pull the brand strategy apart a little bit, and explore all the possibilities inherent in the brand."

Corporate management also plays an important role in the creative process. The same team that worked on the discovery and strategic phases are the "editors" of the creative process. The lead person, however, needs to be the CEO, or someone who at the very least has the CEO's ear . . . and a fluent understanding of the CEO's vision for the brand.

Whether the CEO or another key executive is leading the process, the relationship has to be strong, interactive, and centered on the brand strategy.

"I think the key is that everything we do is going to be based on the strategy," Bogucki says. "The relationship is hugely important, and it has to be based on the fact that we're all working to find the best solution, and it's got to be based on the brand strategy."

CHARTING THE COURSE FOR A NEW IDENTITY

Andrew Bogucki describes the way that a creative exploration developed for an energy company.

"The whole notion," Bogucki says, "was that they're a guide through the energy market. They get you to the right solution and handle this very important and very tricky and volatile part of the business for you.

"Now of course, you have to look at what was going on in the industry at that point. Enron had just fallen apart, so the waters were a little treacherous: People weren't necessarily going to trust an energy company.

"So based on the brand strategy, we developed several possible directions for the brand identity. The first direction we explored was the whole notion of strength, solidity, and conservatism. Whatever we came up with for this bucket had to give the impression that the company was going to stick around.

"The second bucket was about the whole notion of navigation, of charting the course. Thirdly, we explored the idea of equilibrium and balance.

"The fourth—and winning—direction was about repeatability and predictability, and pattern and process. It's a little more abstract, but it reinforced the experience we wanted people to have from this company, of creating order from a chaotic and confusing environment."

FINDING THE "PERFECT" SOLUTION

One of the important lessons we've learned over the years is that there is rarely one perfect solution to the question of creating a brand identity. What's more, no one visual solution can capture every nuance of the brand: This underscores the importance of having every aspect of the corporation live the brand, not just the communications platform.

Karl Barnhart explains, "There's not one solution for any problem or project; there are some that are better than others. I think there are many options that can be perfectly viable solutions, although some will meet the strategic, functional, and aesthetic needs better than others."

Andrew Bogucki adds, "One important thing to keep in mind is that no one identity is going to be able to do everything. You can't capture every single nuance in a visual work, because it's impossible.

"But the visual experience of a brand is hugely important," Bogucki continues. "There are certain images and symbols that mean things to us, that have come to mean something in society. We try to draw from those and create an appropriate identity to which people will respond in the right way."

When companies were less complex, identities were more straightforward. In the 1940s and 1950s, for instance, when AT&T was simply the phone company, their bell logo—harking back to the inventor of the telephone—was an instant signal of their business and corporate brand identity.

In our time, when corporations are in numerous businesses, or in abstract or technical fields, an identity has to convey much more information in a compact and telegraphic way. Once AT&T became an information services company, for example, the bell logo was no longer relevant to their business, and they needed to make a change that suggested global telecommunications.

In the case of another telecom firm, MCI, the logo originally consisted of block letters and a symbolic long-distance line emerging from it. Once MCI became a global provider, that logo represented an old technology, and it made sense to freshen the logo's look.

Bogucki says, "There are very few companies that can be literal anymore. One of the criteria for making a great logo used to be that somebody could look at it and get a good sense of what that company did. But now, so many companies are so diversified, and there are lots of companies that don't make an actual product—they create solutions, they find data, they provide services. That isn't tangible, so we have to create metaphors for what they're doing, and what they plan to continue doing in the future.

"There are some companies, though, that still have a focus," Bogucki continues. "For some smaller companies, it's easier to get a handle on their one key business promise. Even so, we try to keep an eye on where they might go someday. You don't want to give them something that's going to limit their growth as a brand."

Executing the Ideas

Creating a meaningful experience with the brand includes every part of its visual expression.

As Karl Barnhart explains, it includes "the way that you use type, the way you use color, the way that you use the corporate logo or symbol, the way that you design your systems, the way that you use templates, Microsoft Office applications, the way your Web site looks.

"The identity should feed into all of your communications," Barnhart continues, "whatever they might be. From business cards to brochures to ads to Web sites—to trucks and uniforms and everything else in between."

One of the secrets to a good identity is consistency. The brand identity has to be expressed consistently both throughout the organization—with the encouragement of senior management and development of brand guidelines—as well as over time.

Bogucki adds, "When the identity makes sense, and everything's consistent, it creates a powerful message. There will always be those times when the only thing that someone has to react to is a business card, or a brochure, or a home page on the Web. No one from your company has talked to them yet, but they're already forming an opinion of you based on the clues they get from your materials."

The importance of consistent execution and implementation is often underestimated as a part of the creative branding process.

Bogucki explains, "I don't want to see a company with a bad logo. But I'd rather see a company with an okay logo that's implemented really well, than a company with an amazing conceptual, emotional logo that gets implemented inconsistently, or haphazardly.

"You often see companies that have created this new identity and then just hand it off," Bogucki continues, "and all of a sudden all the different agencies that are doing the work for this company are doing whatever they want to do with it. To me, you might as well not have bothered."

At the same time, however, communications alone will not adequately support the company's brand. Barnhart notes that the strategy for the company will indicate how spending on the brand identity should be prioritized.

"In a customer-focused, face-to-face organization," Barnhart says, "you might not necessarily spend a gazillion dollars on a new Web site, for example. But you might spend more time training your sales representatives and giving them tools, such as printed communication, that they can use with prospects."

No matter how your company chooses to express itself, having a strong brand identity provides a critical advantage in competitive markets.

As Andrew Bogucki observes, "If you don't create and implement a strong brand identity, you've missed an opportunity to make your brand strategy visible."

A CASE IN POINT: JETBLUE

Bogucki and Barnhart agree that one of their favorite brand expressions is embodied by JetBlue.

Barnhart defines their business strategy: "We're low-cost, but we're going to give you a pleasant experience.

"They manage your experience," Barnhart continues, "from the time you call the travel agent or go to their Web site, to when you get off the plane at your destination.

"I took JetBlue to Orlando," Barnhart recounts, "and the plane was full of kids on their way to see Mickey. The pilot and the first officer were joking around the whole way down, and the kids on the plane loved it. I've never been on a plane like this before, ever. It was fantastic. Everything was so consistent, so well done, with their identity and the experience they offered. And the experience was the big star."

Bogucki discusses how JetBlue's corporate identity reinforces the experiences it offers.

"What we see is a logo that's very simple, very clean, very basic, and that talks about the nature of the services," Bogucki explains. "This is real straightforward: no frills, but it's also approachable, with the lowercase J, cap B on the airplanes. As simple as that identity is, and as subliminal as some of those messages are, it's saying the right things, and backing up what the company's about."

Barnhart and Bogucki took a moment to imagine how JetBlue could have used their brand attributes—low-cost and friendly—to come up with a completely different type of identity.

"Imagine if they had called the airline Discountarama," Barnhart jokes, "and had a kid draw a plane for it, and used crayons to illustrate their sales materials and their ads."

Bogucki says, "If they had gotten lost in their own underwear and just gone with this idea of being friendly, that could have been harmful. But you're talking about air traffic here. It's got to be solid, stable. It can be approachable and friendly and all those things, but you don't want to get up in the air in an airline that you don't think is professional. And an identity can show that."

Comparing JetBlue's strategy to other airlines with similar brand platforms is also instructive.

Barnhart says, "Compare JetBlue to Spirit airlines: They're also a discount airline, but Spirit has a different business philosophy. They bought older planes, and it's true, they'll get you where you're going, cheap. The business strategy for JetBlue was, we're going to buy brand-new planes, and we want an identity that's brand new, fresh, creative, and consistent with that business philosophy."

Chapter Seven | Step Four: Management

CREATING A BRANDING CULTURE

In addition to developing a platform for corporate communications, the brand strategy provides a framework for creating a corporate branding culture.

All too often, senior management invests a tremendous amount of effort to develop and personify their brand strategy, and then believe they're finished. Nothing could be further from the truth. Those steps are vital to the branding process. But the most important, fundamental thing a company has to do over time is to ensure that the experiences its audiences will get from the company will be consistent with the brand strategy. This is what we call *managing the brand.*

Managing your corporate brand on a long-term basis is truly where the hard work begins. It's where many companies lose heart and don't take care of the asset they've just spent so many hours and dollars defining. A brand is a valuable asset; corporate branding is a long-term initiative, which gains steam as it builds. No matter how much care you take to create your brand, if you don't nurture it and help it grow, it will die and take with it the investment your company has made to date. You will lose all the financial potential you would have realized as a result of having a strong corporate brand.

If you think of your communications as being primarily an external effort, managing the brand is primarily internal. Catherine Ostheimer, CoreBrand's Brand Director, calls this phase "the missing link" in branding.

"You can spend a heck of a lot of money in advertising and creating a new logo," Ostheimer says, "but unless your employees are delivering the brand the right way, it's a waste."

A company with a healthy branding culture is one in which every employee—from the CEO down—not only understands what the brand is about, but understands what their role is in delivering that brand. Never underestimate the importance of your internal audiences: They deliver your brand to the world.

Without that understanding, Ostheimer says, "You get brand discordance. You get people thinking, 'This is not the company I thought it was,' or 'They used to be such a good company, I don't know what happened.' "

"And what probably happened is that one person got one customer service rep on the phone who had a bad day or just forgot about representing the company. It takes so little to break brand loyalty. And how much does it take to build it? A lot."

Ostheimer explains that when a company is properly managing its brand, "Everyone is working off the same page. As soon as you hear the name of a company, you have an immediate impression of them. Look at Ben & Jerry's: Even though they were purchased by a larger company, they kept their strong values about helping society. And everyone in the company shares those values.

"Dell is a company that has all of these things working for it," Ostheimer continues. "They've had some ups and downs, but their brand culture is all about being very direct. Mike Dell is very direct in how he talks to his employees. Their business processes are about selling direct. Their communications have a very direct appeal; if you read the copy it's simple and straightforward. You see how everything lines up. You have a very clear image about what that company is and what it's about. And there are not a lot of surprises."

Relative to a corporation's other business processes, creating a brand culture is not expensive: Often, it's a small percentage of a corporation's advertising budget. Ostheimer reveals that one CoreBrand client, a Fortune 500 company, spent $500,000 on their internal communications and training, "and that's pretty conservative, compared to what some companies are spending just on advertising."

But creating an internal brand culture requires a serious commitment from the CEO and senior management. The reality is that budget and time and effort are required to fulfill the dream and desire for a stronger brand and a successful company. Unfortunately, if companies don't succeed, we often find that the reason is a lack of commitment to the corporate brand, and to the hard work that's required to excel.

THE CEO IS THE STANDARD BEARER

Just as the discovery process begins with the CEO and flows throughout the organization, managing the brand starts at the top. A CEO is not the brand, but he or she is its most prominent representative. As such, his or her role is indispensable in managing the brand.

For the outside world, the CEO is your company's primary spokesperson. Whether it's fair or not, the company will be judged by how smart, articulate, pleasant, powerful, or persuasive the CEO is. Harvey Golub is known as a tough talker; under his aegis American Express began to be perceived as a tougher company than it was under predecessor James Robinson III. Richard Branson has told the world that he is a freewheeling, adventurous, exciting guy, and Virgin is seen to share many of those characteristics, particularly in comparison to its competition.

Larry McNaughton observes that "Some companies, like Microsoft for example, have taken what their CEO is all about and have institutionalized that within the organization. Bill Gates is famous for being a poker player, and the object of the poker player is to take all the chips. Not 27 and a half percent because that's fair, not 73 percent because it's fair, but all of them—because that's the name of the game. And taking all the chips is how Microsoft runs its business."

The CEO is truly the only person in the corporation who can launch an effective brand management initiative. Eventually, the process will encompass an intense effort that will include company-wide training; internal and external communications; even changes in chains of command.

With all this at stake, the branding initiative must be perceived as a high-priority management function, with performance objectives and rewards equal to any major business activity.

Tim Robinson underscores the fact that branding is hard work, but can be done—and is done successfully by some of America's major companies.

"Branding requires a lot of maintenance," Robinson says. "It requires a lot of tension. And some companies, I think, do an excellent job at it. You look at a company like Apple, where everything they do follows their premise of empowering people with technology. Across the board, everyone in the company knows it.

"It requires a strong leader to do it," Robinson continues. "It requires somebody who is going to stand up and take ownership of the brand in the eyes of the world. Generally, it should be the CEO. In some cases, it can be someone else, but the CEO has the credibility in the eyes of all the stakeholders to be that force."

Ostheimer agrees: "People won't believe they have to fall in line unless the CEO says so; that's just the way it is. There's a trickle-down effect. If the CEO says to his immediate staff, 'this brand stuff is a little soft, I don't really believe in it,' eventually that attitude will trickle down, and the brand effort will fall to pieces.

"On the other hand, if the CEO understands the economic value created by branding, and invests in the brand, that attitude will also 'trickle down.' The whole company will become enthusiastic about supporting—and living—the brand."

Make Sure the Brand Is Well Understood throughout Your Organization

More often than not, corporations operate in a very decentralized way, with dispersed and autonomous geographic or business units. Your objective is to get people thinking and talking about one company, with a set of common goals and interests.

Catherine Ostheimer says, "I think too many companies—whether it's because of a new CEO moving in, or people being influenced by someone on the board—have too many strategies de jour. And it leaves employees' heads spinning. They don't know what the vision is for the company. 'What am I supposed to be? How am I supposed to be approaching my job? How should I be setting my goals? How should I be acting on a day-to-day basis?' "

The best way to create a unified branding culture is to institute what we call a Brand Council. This is a group representing various facets of the organization; collectively, they're empowered to centralize brand-based decision making for the company. The Brand Council makes sure that the corporate brand is infused equally throughout different parts of the organization.

The Brand Council oversees the implementation of corporate communications and business processes. It also has the responsibility for making the brand the focal point for shaping how employees behave. Whether your company employs 10 people, 10,000, or 100,000, all of them must deliver the experiences defined by the brand strategy, whether that means delivering outstanding service, a caring attitude, or a keen understanding of the technology you use.

Ultimately, the Brand Council makes sure that employees throughout the company, at every level and in every location, understand the brand. They must understand why it's important to the company, and, more importantly, why it's important to them as individuals, whether they're truck drivers, factory floor workers, or senior vice presidents.

Having a good brand culture can even attract the right kind of people.

Ostheimer says, "At Harley-Davidson there is such a cult-like love for the brand, it can't help but attract and keep a certain kind of employee. And there are a couple of other brands like that, mainly lifestyle brands. Club Med, for instance, attracts a certain type—people with an international mindset, people who want to have fun and meet new people, and are generally happy—people who are consistent with Club Med's brand personality."

Ostheimer notes that an ideal Brand Council includes separate committees focused on culture, business processes, and communications.

"You need to create alignment in a number of diverse areas, and it takes focus. Just to handle the culture, you need to work with human resources and the leadership team," Ostheimer says. "Business processes can run the gamut from customer service, to your financial terms for billing customers, to product development. And communications is more focused on delivering appropriate messages to employees, customers, and vendors."

THREE STEPS TO STRONG BRAND ALIGNMENT

There are three key things that companies with good branding cultures do to create strong internal alignment:

1. *Brand documentation.* When a brand is launched, or relaunched, even before any formal education occurs, the company creates a general awareness that something new is happening. There may be an announcement from the CEO that the strategy is changing, or that a new logo is being unveiled. Typically, at this stage, employees are open but a bit skeptical.

The next step is to create tangible documentation: a brand book, perhaps a video, which talks in detail about the new brand, the brand promise, and brand attributes. These give employees a solid idea of how they're going to start doing their jobs differently, or become more consistent in current practices. These materials should be able to answer employees' most common questions, and underscore both the stability of the new brand and the company's direction for the future. There are a lot of creative ways to document the brand. The idea is to be consistent and get everyone playing by the same rules.

An excellent way to provide brand documentation is via the company Web site. This provides the opportunity to have an easily updateable resource for Internet-enabled employees throughout the organization, in every part of the world where your company does business. (Of course, employees without Web access will still need printed materials to help them understand the new brand guidelines.) Internet-based tools for brand management can be quite extensive, including everything from downloadable artwork, such as logos; to product naming guidelines; to behavioral guidelines for customer service.

2. *Brand training.* Training personalizes the brand for your employees. It gives people at every level the opportunity to understand how the brand applies to them, and how it will affect the way they perform their jobs.

Although training can be done online, live training is usually better, since participants can ask questions and be interactive. It's also true that people tend to retain things better if they're taught in person.

Training ideally includes brand workshops, where all employees can learn about branding basics. In this setting, employees can get a first-hand introduction to the brand, and ask questions, like "Why are we focused on the brand? What is a brand? How did you come up with this brand promise?"

These kinds of workshops make sure that not only the leadership team understands what the brand is about but that all the customer-facing employees do as well. Even people that you wouldn't think are really representatives of the brand every day support people who interact with customers, vendors, and the rest of the outside world, and as a result, must reflect, the brand internally. Everyone needs to know what the brand is all about.

Catherine Ostheimer gives an example of a training program developed for Dun & Bradstreet.

"We created a 4-hour training module for D&B," she reveals. "The first participants were customer-facing associates, but eventually it will be rolled out to all employees. We identified four attributes that comprise the D&B brand and created a video that talks about the attributes in a pretty funny way. We also designed some games to help the participants internalize those four attributes.

"In the last part of the workshop," Ostheimer continues, "the participants work in a team to solve a client need, using the brand attributes and some of the solutions that D&B offers. This way, they make a conscious effort not only to provide the appropriate solution but link it with one of the core brand attributes. That's one way to personalize brand management within your company."

3. *Accountability.* Companies that are successful in living the brand generally create a culture based on merit, where brand-based performance is motivated and rewarded. They create a consistent system in which employees know that they will be measured, promoted, and compensated based on how well they're delivering the brand.

This is where the active participation and management of your HR department is critical. They will need to create and implement a system in which employees are monitored and rewarded, based on a set of standards that is both consistent with the brand and tailored to individual job descriptions. The rewards, whether in the form of time, money, or recognition, need to be consistent with the overall brand; you'll be able to measure the benefit to your corporation in increased employee loyalty as well as improved performance.

As Ostheimer says, "If you have all of your employees aligned and they're all delivering the brand day in and day out, that's going to build customer loyalty. It's only natural that customers are going to trust and want to buy or use a company's products or services if that company is delivering a consistent experience time and time again."

Monitor, Measure, and Make Adjustments

Given the time, expense, and commitment to create and manage a strong brand, it is vital to monitor your brand health on a regular basis. This gives you the opportunity to catch problems before they become systemic, evaluate the success of different aspects of your brand strategy and implementation, and analyze the impact of outside events on your brand.

Virtually every large company thinks that they monitor their brand health. Most of them are wrong. As we discussed briefly in Part 1, many companies run periodic studies on one or more audience segments, one or more products, or some other variable affecting their business. But very few benchmark their brand or their internal branding process. That's the first problem.

The second thing many companies do wrong is use inconsistent methodology. They may have five different companies over 5 years do their research; they may change their questions or research goals year to year; they may skip a year, or two or three.

It is impossible to overestimate the importance of tracking your brand consistently.

Brad Puckey, CoreBrand's Associate Brand Director, explains, "Benchmarking is when you field a study for the first time. Tracking is when you replicate that study time and time again. That's what we've done with our database, the Corporate Branding Index; we use the same methodology, we ask the same questions year after year. So the data we track is comparable year to year and company to company.

"Now if a corporation has three different studies by three different companies," Puckey continues, "the questionnaires aren't even the same. How can you say that you're tracking if you don't have anything in this time period that was comparable to a previous time period? It's ultimately very expensive, very time-consuming, and never gives you a good picture of how your brand is changing over time. It's very rare to find a company that has a program that's been stable."

The most effective way to monitor your brand is to combine consistent real-world research with the use of quantitative models to measure, and even predict, changes in key variables.

For the internal brand analysis, Catherine Ostheimer recommends an online or telephone survey to get feedback from your employees, customers, and other audience segments.

"You take a reading to see how well people understand the brand platform and its important attributes," Ostheimer says. "Then in 6 months you do it again to see how much you moved the needle. And every 6 months you do another survey to see how much things change as a result of training, communications, changing the way people are rewarded and promoted.

"Corporate Express did a benchmark of how familiar their employees were with the corporate brand," Ostheimer continues. "After the first study, they went out to all of their offices and educated their employees about the brand and how the brand platform could be integrated into their jobs. Six months later, they went back and repeated the study. Sure enough, where 20 percent of the employees understood the brand before, after the training program the number was 89 percent. It shows that their program was successful in educating their employees."

The second tool to monitor the brand is a computer model that can track and correlate your company's benchmarks over time. Your model can track any one of a number of goals: The question for each company is, how do you define success? For a small company, this might mean breaking into the next level of competition; for a private company, it might be increased revenue; for a large, publicly held corporation it might be an increase in stock price or valuation.

"For instance," Puckey says, "someone could say, 'My goal is to improve my brand and have an impact on my stock performance.' So the model would look at how communicating at different spending levels would affect your brand, and how that in turn will affect stock price. And then we can look at how much you have to spend to affect your stock price and make sure that the growth in stock price is going to offset how much you spend on communications."

The model also serves as an important reality check. As we discussed in Chapter 2, measurements such as the Advertising Efficiency Curve can determine whether your company is spending too much—or too little—on its corporate communications.

As Puckey says, "You may have somebody in the organization saying, 'I'm going to increase revenue by 25 percent in 3 years.' It's possible that we would look at the data and realize it's just not going to happen unless they spend $100 million on advertising. And by the way, the last $10 million will only get you a tiny fraction of what the first $10 million got. So spending $100 million may get you where you want to be, but it may not be all that much more effective than, say, $50 million. And that $50 million may take you most of the way toward your goal."

And just as we did at the beginning of the process, we continue to monitor the company's CoreBrand Power. The use of our analytic intelligence allows us to see the impact of the brand strategy—and brand management—on the company's current CoreBrand Power rating, its stock price, price to earnings ratio (P/E), valuation, and how it's faring in comparison with its competitors.

The health of your corporate brand is a prime indicator of the health of your company—including future sales, employee retention, and stock valuation.

As Larry McNaughton says, "If I were your brand doctor, I would say, keep an eye on your brand body all the time. And if you see any anomalies, anything weird occurring, give me a call. In the meantime, I want you to have an annual checkup. Absolutely, there's no question."

And Now?

The process doesn't end here. Rather, it loops right back to the beginning, with an ongoing process of discovery.

Your brand is something that should stand the test of time. Of course, it should be tweaked as marketplace changes occur, but it is something that should live for 10, 20 years, or more. During that time, management will change, the investment climate will change, products and services will change.

If you use your brand as a focal point, your company will ride all those waves and become even stronger over time.

PART THREE
The 12 Best Practices in Corporate Branding . . . Inside Some of America's Smartest Brands

Chapter Eight | Best Practice No. 1

Have a Vision

here was no reason to suppose, looking back at the early 1990s, that American Express would still be around a decade later, much less that it would continue to enjoy a thriving business in charge and credit cards, as well as other financial services.

Back then, American Express was in the grip of a corporate arrogance so strong that it believed, as if it were a landmark or national monument, that people would simply continue to come to it. But the rest of the industry was hungrier and harder-working and produced innovations that left American Express a ripe target for takeover or worse.

Enter CEO Harvey Golub and his partner—later successor—Ken Chenault. Together, they formed and implemented a vision of American Express that was relevant, exciting, and still allowed the company to command a premium price.

The success of their strategies is obvious in the company's improved CoreBrand Power and other measures. Even in the wake of the terrorist attacks that directly affected their core business of travel and entertainment—as well as the very building that houses their

New York headquarters—Golub and now Chenault's vision has sustained American Express as one of the country's, and the world's, premier corporate brands.

> *A brand establishes an expectation, a promise you make of a relationship.*
>
> —John Hayes, Executive Vice President,
> Global Advertising and Brand Management,
> American Express Company

AMERICAN EXPRESS
A VISION FROM THE TOP

The year 2001 was one of the most difficult years on record for American Express. Salomon Smith Barney summed up the reasons in its 2001 end-of-year research report: "A softer economy brought weaker corporate T&E spending and a deteriorating credit environment. . . . An equity bear market hurt performance in the company's asset management business. . . . The events of September 11 resulted in the company evacuating its New York headquarters, as well as exacerbating an already weak economy."

American Express, the report continued, "has been through countless iterations of product portfolio and corporate structure, but, throughout, has retained one of the strongest brands in financial services history."

Despite the challenges of 2001, Salomon Smith Barney's rating was 1M: buy.

In his remarks to the financial community in February 2002, Chairman and CEO Ken Chenault agreed that, in terms of financial results, "2001 was clearly a disappointment."

Yet despite the setbacks of the economy and the effects of terrorism on travel and entertainment spending—not to mention the partial destruction of the company's own New York City headquarters—Chenault was able to point to encouraging signs. Consumer billings were up 6 percent for the year, and the company was up 13 percent in lending balances.

But 2001 was not the hardest year American Express ever had, by far. The fact that it has survived is a credit to the power of the brand and the vision of its most recent leaders.

American Express was created as a delivery service in 1850; among its principals were Henry Wells and William Fargo, who later spun off a separate delivery service for the state of California. In 1882, American Express introduced a money order, followed by the introduction of Travelers' Cheques in 1891.

The company opened its first overseas office in Paris in 1895; in 1919, it created an international bank to serve its customers outside the United States.

As Ken Chenault would later describe the evolution of the business, "We started out as an express company. We moved goods. And then money."

In World War I, the American government nationalized all express delivery services; American Express reinvented itself, offering overseas freight, financial services, and currency exchange. It wasn't until 1958 that the company introduced what is now its signature product—the American Express Card.

James D. Robinson III became CEO of the company in 1977. His dream was to turn American Express into a financial services superpower—or at least supermarket. To do that, he embarked on a series of acquisitions, starting with the brokerage firm Shearson Loeb Rhodes in 1981. This was followed by the purchase of financial planner Investors Diversified Services (IDS) and investment bankers Lehman Brothers in 1984.

But by 1993, the company was in serious trouble. In a speech at Howard University, Ken Chenault recalled that during the early 1990s he "would shudder" each time he opened the *Wall Street Journal* or *New York Times* because of the constant headlines about problems at AmEx. In fact, Chenault declared, "We almost fell off the cliff as a business."

The company had two systemic problems. It had become a holding company for Shearson Lehman, IDS, and others, but losses in the early 1990s drove AmEx earnings dramatically downward. In addition, AmEx had introduced its first revolving credit card product, the

Optima Card, in 1987, but with no experience underwriting credit cards, they were badly burned by losses in this area as well.

Worst, its signature business, the American Express Card, was in a tailspin. Between 1983 and 1992, AmEx's share of the U.S. card market dropped from 26.5 to 19.9 percent. Over the same period, Visa International's share grew from 43.3 to 46.1 percent.

The basic Personal Card cost consumers a hefty $55 per year, and of course, required payment in full each month. By contrast, banks had begun offering low or no fee Visa and MasterCards; price competition was further spurred when Capitol Bank began offering consumers lower interest rates on their card products. Merchants paid less to use bank cards too, with a lower transaction fee than the 3.5 percent per purchase that American Express demanded. Although bank cards didn't have the "elite" status that an American Express card seemed to confer, they offered consumers what they wanted: low prices and opportunities to use their cards virtually anywhere they shopped.

Joan Solotar, an analyst at Donaldson, Lufkin & Jenrette Securities Corp., told *Investor's Business Daily* that "American Express is probably in one of the worst competitive positions. They're at the high end of a price-sensitive market that is expensive to both cardholders and merchants."

And yet, Robinson and his team were doing little to avert the growing crisis. One senior executive revealed to *Fortune* that, among management, "there was a feeling that American Express was an elite product and that we didn't have to stoop to do the things that others did to sell the product."

AmEx's CoreBrand Power illustrates the growing turmoil leading up to 1993, when the company's favorability attributes can be seen to plunge. The spread in attributes start as early as 1991, reflecting the market's gradual decline in confidence in then-CEO Robinson. You can see AmEx's historical CoreBrand performance in Figures 8-1, 8-2, and 8-3.

In 1993, under pressure, James Robinson resigned as CEO. He was replaced by former IDS and McKinsey executive Harvey Golub.

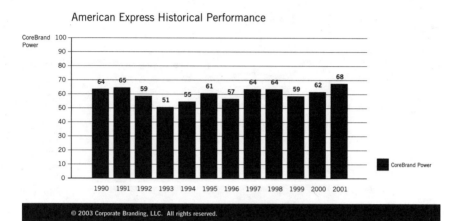

Figure 8-1. CoreBrand Power 1990–2001, American Express Historical Performance

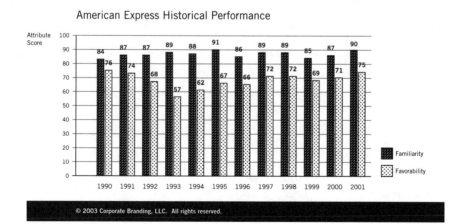

Figure 8-2. Familiarity and Favorability 1990–2001, American Express Historical Performance

Favorability Attributes 1990 - 2001

American Express Historical Performance

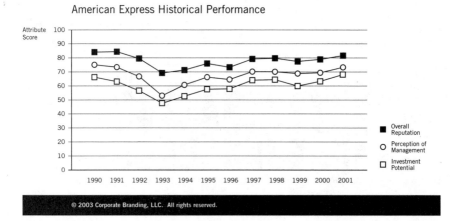

Figure 8-3. Favorability Attributes 1990–2001, American Express Historical Performance

Golub made it his priority to streamline the company: to decide what it was and what it was not. Companies not fitting the updated definition were jettisoned; those that remained were consolidated under the American Express name.

In his 1994 Letter to Shareholders, Golub articulated his strategy: "Our focus on the brand means that our business must be consistent with the attributes our customers associate with the American Express brand . . . and that each business use the brand as an integral part of its strategy."

Golub formulated three key operating principles for the redefined company. The "new" American Express would deliver

- Best-in-class economics
- World-class value and service
- A brand enhanced by every product and service offered

As John Hayes, Executive Vice President, Global Advertising and Brand Management, recalled for us, "At that time, when Harvey articulated those three operating principles, he also articulated that we were not going to be a holding company, we were going to be an operating company. He got the company out of a passive mode, and put the brand in a more active role."

To do that, the single biggest strategic challenge Golub faced was to increase the relevance of the American Express brand. One of the first actions he took was not immediately noticeable to customers at all. Under Robinson's management, working at American Express had included a number of lavish perks; it was a place where, like its famous ad slogan, "membership had its privileges."

Golub began to align the internal company culture with his vision of AmEx as a tough competitive player. Almost immediately, he promoted AmEx veteran Ken Chenault to head U.S. Travel Services, making him responsible for the entire U.S. card business. Chenault had had a number of successes inside American Express, including the introduction of Membership Miles in 1991, but in partnership with Golub, he would soon be instrumental in transforming the company.

Golub and Chenault started setting hard financial targets—and insisted on reaching them. The free-spending executive lifestyle of the 1980s was reined in, and, most shocking to observers, the company began to expand its merchant base beyond the traditional pool of travel and entertainment retailers. Soon merchants from Wal-Mart to the corner gas station would be open for business to customers using their American Express cards.

The strategy worked: Between 1992 and 1996, net income increased 200 percent. New merchant acquisition increased from 100,000 a year to 500,000. Between 1994 and 1996, cards in circulation started rising again . . . increasing almost 4 million in those 2 years alone. AmEx's CoreBrand Power also recovered, climbing from a low of 51 in 1993 to 61 in 1995, a 20 percent improvement.

As the company refined its definition of what American Express stood for, the next challenge was to communicate that message to the world of customers and prospects. The company explored a number of different approaches until they came up with the key: start with the customer.

Starting with the customer . . . means listening to the customer. John Hayes remembers when the company started exploring how to change consumers' perceptions of the American Express card.

"We did a lot of focus groups. We learned that while customers readily used their American Express cards for travel and dining purchases, they did not feel comfortable using their cards in everyday locales such as grocery and hardware stores.

"We said, we have to change this perception. Because we want our customers to feel comfortable using it for all their payment needs."

John Hayes explains how the company arrived at a strategy of focusing on people, rather than products: "We did some work back in the mid-1990s, which was designed to show the scope of American Express: It's financial services, Travelers' Cheques, travel, cards."

"It did change the perception of the brand, because people said, 'Well, it's not just a green card.' But it didn't close the loop enough for them. They said, 'Okay, American Express is being redefined, but I don't know if that's better or worse than what they were.'"

"What we've found more effective," he continues, "is to help the consumer in key areas—customers in the card business, small businesses, customers of American Express financial advisors—to understand how American Express is relevant to them. Because one of the key measures of brand success is increased marketplace demand."

"We ensure that the product attributes—service and trust—are embedded in the product experience as much as in the advertising," Hayes says, "because it's our belief that the product experience actually reinforces and builds the brand as much as the ads do. But we also make sure it's part of all of the communications. We always try to say, 'Here's why this product is relevant to you,' by creating relevant value propositions for different groups, clearly attaching the attributes of the brand to those value propositions and sending it to those segments of the population."

As Hayes notes, creating a relevant brand proposition is about more than just advertising. In fact, American Express has come up with some creative relationship-building efforts that have no immediate impact on sales, but help build the long-term value of the brand.

In the 2000 presidential election, for instance, AmEx saw an opportunity to support its small business owner constituency by helping to get their issues onto the presidential agenda. The company set up a Web site to gather input from small business owners and managers, learning that their key issues included the minimum wage and healthcare. Then, working with *Time* magazine, AmEx was able to have these issues included in editorial coverage of the election.

The company also sponsored town hall–style meetings with small business owners, which were televised on CNN. As Hayes says, "We didn't endorse a candidate in this area. We were merely trying to help small businesses have a voice in what's going on in this country today."

And of course, Hayes adds, "We wanted to increase our relevance to that audience and help them understand that we have a dedicated unit that's here to help small businesses."

Values and relevance also play a part in the company's famous national campaigns. The company has long relied on celebrities to enhance its aura of prestige, but again, under Golub and Chenault, the message was subtly changed. Celebrities are still an important part of AmEx communications, but now, rather than relying on their fame alone, AmEx aligns itself with celebrities whose values represent what the brand stands for—or wants to stand for.

One example of the new values, Hayes explains, is the notion of "earned success." Part of the Golub-Chenault strategy to broaden the appeal of the brand was making card membership less about empty prestige and more about being a reward for hard work. The challenge was to find the celebrity spokesperson who would define that value and bring it to life.

Hayes says, "We see Tiger Woods as someone who stands for earned success. This is a guy who's at the end of the third day of a tournament, and he's ahead by seven strokes, but he's the only guy out in the dark on the driving range. There's that sense of earned success." Figure 8-4 shows one of the Tiger Woods ads.

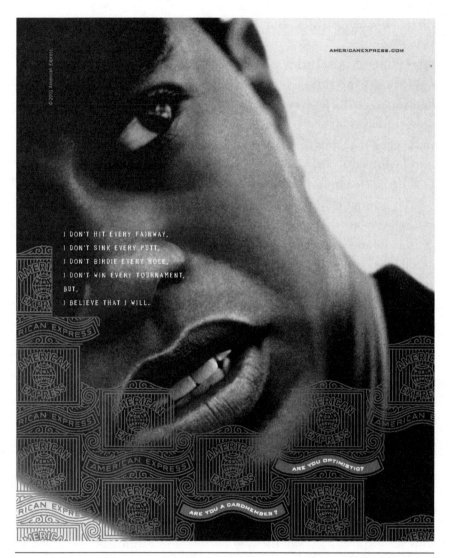

Figure 8-4. Tiger Woods embodies the idea of "earned success" in this American Express card ad. (Used with permission of American Express TRS Company, Inc.)

Another key player in AmEx advertising has been Jerry Seinfeld. Jerry first appeared in a series of commercials underscoring AmEx's increased availability at such everyday locations as hardware stores and gas stations.

Hayes explains, "We said, who better than Jerry Seinfeld to make everyday things interesting? So we took that idea, and over the last 5 or 6 years, Jerry has been helping us change the perception of the brand, overall, in terms of its formality. It helps to relax the brand a little bit. It's still premium quality. It's still prestigious. But it's a little less formal."

One of the company's most prominent achievements recently has been the introduction of Blue. Launched in 1999, the card was designed to help AmEx attract a younger and more tech-savvy audience than its existing charge card base. It was also seen as a way to add more revolving-credit customers to the franchise, since the 12-year-old Optima had never taken off as a credit-card powerhouse.

Blue was also AmEx's entry into e-marketing. The card contained a "smart chip" created to provide greater convenience and security for online transactions. As an added incentive for general use, Blue was brought out with a 0 percent APR, peaking at 9.99 percent after 6 months.

John Hayes says, "When we started to launch Blue, we said, we want to go after a new segment with a new credit card. We wanted it to be unique."

But in addition to being a unique card for a new segment, the product had to share some fundamental values with the corporate brand. The process began with defining the values of the original card—and coming up with a surprising observation.

As Hayes recalls, "One of the things we realized was that the charge card was the original affinity card. There's a lot of affinity card marketing going on today, but it's usually borrowed affinity—so, if you're part of the AMA, there is a product for you. But the charge card was the original affinity product, and we created the affinity—in other words, membership. If you share these values, you can be part of the club."

But the new challenge the company faced was how to extend beyond this affinity. There were other groups of consumers who didn't buy into all of the traditional values American Express espoused, but would be valuable customers. Could the company create another type of affinity?

"We spoke to consumers in April and May of 1999, so you've got to think back," Hayes recalls. "Y2K was coming. And we saw people polarizing into two groups. One said, I think the future is going to be great. Technology, the Internet, wireless, it's all happening. It's going to be fabulous.

"The other group was saying, after I leave here today, I'm going to buy a generator. Because the lights are going to go out. They may never come back on. I'm not flying for a month around January 1st. And I'm keeping cash at home, because the ATMs are all going to shut down. Two very different mindsets."

The audience for the new Blue had crystallized.

Hayes continues, "This Blue notion is really for the people who said, the future is going to be great. Then the product features had to fit that affinity.

"So we had to align it, put the chip on it. But it was about creating a new affinity within the American Express brand. It shared the same values with American Express, but it made those values a little different for the Blue group, appealing to a new segment."

One of the original Blue ads is shown in Figure 8-5.

Figure 8-5. This Blue ad was designed to attract a younger, hipper audience for revolving credit. (Used with permission of American Express TRS Company, Inc.)

AmEx introduced Blue with a wide-ranging campaign that surrounded its target audience with messages on everything from billboards to popcorn bags. In addition, it created a strong musical affinity, recruiting stars from Eric Clapton to Sheryl Crow for promotional concerts, the campaign was kicked off with a free concert in New York City's Central Park. It was the most integrated campaign the company had ever created, in partnership with its long-time agencies Ogilvy & Mather, SiegelGale, Digitas, and Momentum Worldwide.

John Hayes recalls, "When we launched Blue, we spent a lot of time trying to focus on creating an integrated experience for customers and prospects. We wanted prospects to understand what it was like to be a Blue customer even before they became a Blue customer. The more we could give them the sense of that experience, the more they would be compelled to get the product, to take action.

"So we did a number of things," Hayes continues, "to indicate to the audience that we understand who they are, their values, and that we have a product that's right for them. We extended ourselves, not just from a two-dimensional advertising standpoint, but from a three-dimensional experience standpoint.

"Advertising did play a big role," Hayes says. "But also advertising in places you wouldn't expect. For example, we put the Blue message on water bottles throughout the country in health clubs. On popcorn bags in movie theaters. But we also did things like the concert in Central Park, with the kind of musicians that this group would find appealing. And we broadcast it on Fox."

The card was a hit—a big hit. After just 15 months on the market, there were 1.5 million Blue cards in consumer wallets. Even Richard Fairbank, CEO of rival Capital One, was impressed. He told *Fortune* that "Amex is really picking up speed to become arguably the most powerful financial services brand out there."

By 2000, AmEx's CoreBrand Power was once again on an upward climb. Although it has not achieved the levels it enjoyed over a decade ago, its CoreBrand Power is as high or higher than its peer group, and considerably higher than competitive card issuers such as Bank One and Citigroup.

Hayes feels that Wall Street understands what American Express is doing to build its business and its brand. He says, "I think that those who follow our company acknowledge that we put a lot into managing the brand. And they refer to the brand as being a key asset of American Express.

"So I think that the brand and the work that we do at American Express in building the brand is recognized by the Street."

But the most important relationship American Express has is with its customers. As Hayes says, "The brand is really nothing more than the relationship: the value of the relationship, the strength of the relationship. And in that relationship are expectations, and, of course, delivery of expectations.

"When we look at customer satisfaction, we get a tremendous view of how strong the brand is," he continues. And then we look at things like attrition rates on our products. Are people staying with us? And, if not, why not? Do our products exist in the market at a price premium? And can they continue to sustain that price premium as well as they could a year or two ago? The customer satisfaction really measures how well we're doing. And the business results dimensionalize how that turns into increased demand in the marketplace."

After almost a decade of close partnership with Harvey Golub, Ken Chenault became CEO of American Express in January 2001. Under Chenault's leadership, the brand remains positioned to increase revenues, increase the company's international presence, move more aggressively into Web marketing, and keep the brand buzz strong.

"Brands live in people's minds," Chenault has said. "People may not be aware of it or consciously guided by it, but the brand is there, affecting their decisions. The brand is an unspoken covenant, a promise to deliver, an expectation to fulfill. It is an emotional contract that creates a bond with the customer. Without this relationship, we would start from zero every day."

Notes

"American Express Company," Company Capsule, Hoover's Online, www.hoovers.com.

"American Express to Alter Marketing Plan," *The San Diego Union-Tribune*, March 15, 1993.

"AmEx Takes the Cobranding Plunge," *Credit Card Management*, Dec. 1, 1995.

"AXP: Initiating Coverage of AXP with a Buy Rating," American Express Co., Salomon Smith Barney, Dec. 13, 2001.

"Fool Sells AXP," Rule Breaker Portfolio, The Motley Fool, Aug. 11, 1995, www.fool.com

"Humming Along Again," *Credit Card Management*, Aug. 1, 1995.

Interview: John Hayes, Executive Vice President, Global Advertising and Brand Management, American Express Company, by Jim Gregory, August 23, 2001.

Cynthia Aquila, "What's in a Brand?," *Context*, Nov./Dec. 1999.

Kathleen M. Berry, "How American Express Plans to Regain Its Status," *Investor's Business Daily*, March 7, 1994.

Anthony Bianco, "A Talk with Harvey Golub of AmEx," *BusinessWeek Online*, Dec. 11, 2000.

Ken Chenault and Ed Gilligan, "Financial Community Presentation," Corporate Information, American Express, http://home3.americanexpress.com/corp/corpinfo.

Ken Chenault, "Reinventing the Corporation," Remarks given at Howard University, Oct. 11, 1996.

Kevin T. Higgins, "The Centurion's Hesitant Smile," *Credit Card Management*, May 1, 1994.

Joel Hoekstra, "Power Under Pressure," Northwest Airlines *World Traveler*, March 2001.

Mike McNamee, Don't Leave Home without a Freebie," *BusinessWeek Online*, Nov. 8, 1999.

Scot J. Paltrow, "American Express to Spin Off Lehman Bros.," *Los Angeles Times*, Jan. 25, 1994.

Nelson D. Schwartz, "What's in the Cards for AmEx?," *Fortune*, Jan. 22, 2001.

Kelly Shermach, "Rock Continues to Roll in AmEx Blue Promotion," *Card Marketing*, Vol. 3, No. 10, Nov. 1999.

Rob Wells, "American Express Struggles to Revive Card," *The Boston Globe*, Sept. 27, 1993.

Chapter Nine | Best Practice No. 2

Create an Emotional Bond with Customers

Generations of American kids have grown up with the comforting tastes of Campbell's Soup. Generations of moms have used Campbell's Cream of Mushroom to liven up tuna casserole and other dishes.

All that experience gives new meaning to the old adage that the way to people's hearts is through their stomachs: For most of the twentieth century Campbell's Soup was a much-loved addition to the American kitchen.

But recent years have changed the picture for Campbell. Their franchise as a convenience food has been eroded by a myriad of other products, and sales in the soup category—while they never went away—flattened out.

In the 1990s, the company tried to enliven and update its image with expensive new ad campaigns, but instead of increasing sales, the campaigns bombed spectacularly. By 2000, Campbell realized that its brand strength lay exactly in its strong brand heritage . . . and that the emotional attachment consumers had with the brand may have been dormant, but was certainly not gone.

It was that realization that made Campbell's brand, once again, piping hot.

> *Long-term wealth building is the outcome of having passionate and dedicated consumers.*
> —David W. Johnson, former Campbell President and CEO

CAMPBELL SOUP COMPANY
GOING BACK TO "M'M! M'M! BASICS!"

Check your kitchen cabinet. If you're like most Americans, there's at least one can of Campbell's Soup in the cupboard. If it isn't Chicken Noodle, it might be Tomato, or perhaps Cream of Mushroom.

Campbell is a grand old brand. Its condensed soup was one of the first convenience foods: You just had to add water, heat, and eat. The brand was immortalized by artist Andy Warhol, who claimed to eat a can of Campbell's soup every day for lunch. But what is its brand promise in a world of hundreds of convenience foods, fast food, and take-out? What's more, for a company that also owns Godiva, Pepperidge Farm, and other famous names, what is the Campbell brand about if it's not just soup?

Campbell Soup Company is the biggest soup maker in the world, selling more than 500 kinds of soup in 122 countries, from classic Chicken Noodle in the U.S., to Tomato Noodle in Australia, to Watercress with Duck-Gizzard in China. The company owns over 70 percent of the U.S. "wet-soup" market and is Europe's leading soup maker.

But recent times have been tough for the venerable brand. The soup category has been essentially flat, with only 2 percent growth between 1999 and 2000. Even so, Campbell's market share in that same period declined 0.2 percent.

Campbell still operates out of its headquarters in Camden, New Jersey, where the company was founded over 130 years ago as the Joseph A. Campbell Preserve Company. Fruit vendor Joseph Campbell teamed up with icebox maker Abram Anderson to can and preserve fruits, vegetables, and meats. When Anderson left the company in 1876, Arthur Dorrance stepped in as Campbell's new partner. When Campbell himself retired in 1894, the Dorrance family continued to run the company, while keeping the well-known name. Over a century later, the family still retains 54 percent of the company stock.

In 1897, Arthur Dorrance reluctantly hired his nephew John as a company scientist. Arthur did his best to make the offer unattractive: John had to provide his own laboratory equipment and was given a token salary of only $7.50 a week. But the hire proved fateful. It was John, a trained chemist, who figured out how to condense soups, making them more economical to pack, store, and distribute.

The innovation allowed Campbell to sell 10-ounce cans of condensed soups for a dime each, versus the 30 cents charged by its competition for 32 ounces of "uncondensed" soup. Condensed soups were also easier to ship around the country, and the country liked what it tasted.

One of the first soups to be condensed was Campbell's Tomato, introduced to the world in 1897, and still a top seller. By 1911, Campbell was a nationally distributed brand—one of the first companies to achieve that milestone.

The company consolidated its position as the country's leading soup maker in 1915, buying Franco-American, the oldest soup company in the country. By 1922, Campbell's soup was so popular that the company formally adopted "Soup" as its middle name.

Another way that Campbell led the market was with its vision of its consumer. In 1904, long before the women's movement, Campbell began to target its products to working mothers, women who wanted to provide tasty, nutritional food for their children, but didn't have time to cook every meal themselves. You can see a vintage ad in Figure 9-1.

A chance moment led to the creation of Campbell's famous label. In 1898, college football fan and Campbell exec Herberton Williams attended a game between the University of Pennsylvania and Cornell University.

The Cornell team wore bright red and white uniforms. Williams' enthusiasm for the color scheme was formidable enough to convince management at Campbell to change the label to a color scheme that endures on Campbell's classic line of soups to this day.

Figure 9-1. The soup all America loves most of all. (Courtesy of Campbell Soup Company.)

The result was the invention of the Campbell's Kids, the chubby animated characters who have been updated, if not aged, in the past hundred years. The Kids made their debut in trolley-car ads; in the following decades, the Kids survived almost every social trend, up to and including rap. Today, the Campbell's Kids are no longer illustrations, but real-life kids, enjoying soup as a healthy part of their daily lives.

Campbell has also long offered working moms help in the kitchen. In 1916, the company published "Help for the Hostess," a collection of recipes which used condensed soups to liven up "regular" fare. Today, Campbell continues to offer recipes in millions of cookbooks as well as on its Campbellkitchens.com Web site. As a result, Americans are still cooking with soup—buying more than 440 million cans every year to use in everything from Green Bean Casserole to Glorified Chicken. Campbell's condensed soups are the fourth most popular ingredient (behind meat or poultry, pasta, and seasonings) used to prepare dinner every night. You can take a look at one soup-inspired recipe in Figure 9-2.

The company began to move beyond soup after World War II. After buying V8 juice in 1948, the company acquired such other well-known brands as Swanson's (1955), Pepperidge Farm (1961), Godiva Chocolatier (1966), and Vlasic Pickles (1978).

Speaking to us recently, John Faulkner, Campbell's Director of Brand Communications, says, "Perhaps the biggest branding challenge we have is that our brand portfolio goes well beyond soup, yet our most popular brand, Campbell, is so closely linked to our corporate brand, Campbell Soup Company.

"It's an ongoing challenge," Faulkner continues, "to appropriately manage the Campbell brand in categories where it has natural equities, while also supporting our other powerful brand trademarks in categories where they can compete and grow. Godiva has achieved its own brand persona and prominence. It's built very discretely from Campbell. Pepperidge Farm is another powerful brand franchise. To the consumer, there's very little connection to Campbell Soup Company, but to investors interested in our corporate brand, we certainly try to link Campbell with these brands."

Figure 9-2. The Campbell's Kids evolved from illustrated tastemakers to real kids enjoying Campbell's soup. The ad shown here, from 2002, continues the decades-long Campbell's tradition of providing recipes for busy moms. (Courtesy of Campbell Soup Company.)

Faulkner says that while Campbell's corporate advertising is limited to its Web site, annual report, and investor meetings, "Campbell's Soup is our most powerful brand, and it's also our corporate name. I think those people who need to know have a good understanding of how to connect the dots between Campbell Soup Company and our other powerful brands." The cover of Campbell's 2001 Annual Report, illustrating the diversity of its brands, is shown in Figure 9-3.

But the 1990s were a period of declining sales for Campbell's soups: Growth came from raising prices, not increasing volume. Even though the company sold its 20 billionth can of condensed tomato soup in January 1990, consumers were drifting to other convenient meals and snacks.

While the company clearly needed to take action to beef up its brand image, the sentimental attachment consumers have for the Campbell brand runs deep, making updating the brand image a tricky proposition.

In 1999, Campbell introduced a new ad campaign, with the tagline "We have a soup for that." The campaign was intended to show how Campbell's soups fit into a variety of lifestyles. Like the campaign before it, "Good for the body, good for the soul," also from ad agency BBDO, the ads bombed: sales declined 2 percent while the ads were running. The *Wall Street Journal* called the campaign a $95 million flop.

BBDO Vice Chairman and Chief Creative Officer Ted Sann was quoted in *Ad Age* about the difficulties of changing a beloved brand: "We've run into difficulty because Campbell Soup's strong brand heritage was almost antithetical to changing it for today."

Even though Campbell still enjoyed nearly 70 percent of the condensed soup market, Wall Street analysts were concerned about the company's failure to build the brand. Then-President and CEO Dale Morrison pushed aside the classic brands, cutting spending for advertising and product development in favor of new product introductions, including ready-to-serve Soup to Go! and growing popular but smaller lines, like Chunky and Simply Home. Unfortunately, none of those lines could grow fast enough to make up for the decline in condensed soup sales.

It's not enough to be a legend.

Figure 9-3. Artist Andy Warhol created an enduring pop icon from the venerable Campbell brand. (Courtesy of Campbell Soup Company.)

In March 2000, Morrison resigned, having failed to meet financial targets for three successive quarters. By the time of his departure, the company's market value had eroded by 50 percent.

Not everyone was convinced Morrison was the problem. An article on the Motley Fool Web site said that "Dale Morrison probably isn't to blame . . . He 'inherited' a difficult selling environment for soup the past three years. [In addition], Campbell's management was busy divesting the company of many underperforming divisions and acquiring international soup leaders, rather than being altogether focused on growing sales."

The article continued: "When a company tries many initiatives to improve its stock's performance, though, and it just doesn't work, eventually shareholders will demand significant change. Whether or not Dale Morrison is responsible for Campbell's woes . . . shareholders wanted change, and changing the CEO was the largest change possible."

Morrison was replaced, on a temporary basis, by former CEO David Johnson, who promised to "go back to basics." On September 6, 2000, a few months after Johnson's return, Campbell went back to basics in its advertising as well. For the first time in 16 years, consumers heard the old familiar jingle with the words so many had grown up with: "M'm! M'm! Good!"

Faulkner reflects, "The M'm! M'm! Good! jingle was one of the top ten ad slogans of the twentieth century, yet we hadn't used it overtly in our advertising for 16 years. Nevertheless, whenever we said 'M'm! M'm! Good!' to consumers, they'd respond—'Campbell's Soup!' Even more powerful, when we'd say, 'Campbell's Soup' to consumers, their first association was most often 'M'm! M'm! Good!' It just made sense to utilize this classic jingle, while at the same time updating and contemporizing the look and feel of our advertising."

In addition to the famous jingle, the ads delivered "new news" from the familiar brand. For example, one ad highlighted the benefits of Campbell's most popular and classic products: the health benefits of Tomato soup, the addition of 20 percent more chicken to Campbell's Chicken Noodle soup, the ease of cooking with Campbell's Cream of Mushroom soup. The ads also promoted a new line of ready-to-serve soups, as well as the 30 varieties of Campbell's condensed soups with fewer than 100 calories and less than 3 grams of fat per serving.

The budget for the campaign represented a significant increase in spending, as the company focused on building value for its icon brand: the classic soups in the red and white labels, which together make up almost half of Campbell's condensed soup sales.

The increase in spending, and the return of M'm! M'm! Good!, helped increase Campbell's soup business by 5 percent. It also inspired a new attention to ad spending on Campbell's nonsoup brands, including V8, Pepperidge Farm, Prego Pasta Sauces, and Franco-American SpaghettiO's.

The new campaign, and the increased ad spending, coincided with product and packaging innovation. The company introduced easy-open packaging for all 70 varieties of its ready-to-serve soups and introduced new soup flavors across these lines.

F. Martin Thrasher, Campbell's President of North America Soup and Sauce, said that "Campbell Soup Company has a stable of powerful brands and none is more powerful than our Campbell's soup brand . . . Making our great soups even more convenient is a key element of our soup strategy."

Faulkner believes that technology will enhance taste as well as convenience: "In 2000 we put pop-tops on all of our ready-to-serve soups. We've announced that we'll roll this innovation out over the next couple of years to our condensed soup varieties, as well.

"In addition, we're making a significant investment in our plants that will enable us to prepare our soups so that their flavor, texture, and taste are significantly improved," Faulkner adds. "The technology investment that is required is one we don't think our competitors will want to make. Consumers will taste a real difference in quality between Campbell's soups and others on the market."

Campbell's CoreBrand Power rating reflects its "back-to-basics" strategy and increased ad spending. Back in 1990, when spending against the brand was less than $60 million, and ad messages were unpopular, Campbell's CoreBrand Power was 61. Between 1996 and 1998, when brand spending had increased to an average of about $100 million per year, its CoreBrand Power rose to 72. See the graph in Figure 9-4.

CoreBrand Power 1990 - 2001

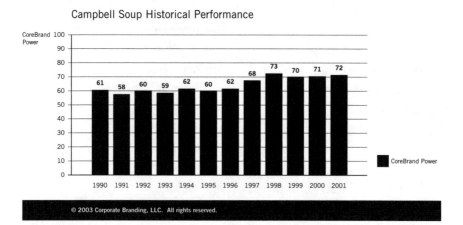

Campbell Soup Historical Performance

© 2003 Corporate Branding, LLC. All rights reserved.

Figure 9-4. CoreBrand Power 1990–2001, Campbell Soup Historical
Performance

A decline in ad spending in 1999—from $108 to $90 million—precipitated a drop in CoreBrand Power. However, the return of "M'm! M'm! Good!" in 2000 made up for lower spending by pushing up the company's familiarity ratings to an incredible 92 . . . and bringing its CoreBrand Power back up to 71, as shown in Figure 9-5.

Campbell's current CoreBrand Power rating makes it the leader in its category. Faulkner explains this by saying that "people are familiar with Campbell and are favorable to Campbell for many reasons. The fact is, something like 98 percent of the public has grown up using our brand." See Figure 9-6 for a comparison of CoreBrand Power among Campbell's peer group.

But the CoreBrand Power rating more likely reflects what Faulkner calls the "emotional attachment" people have with the Campbell Soup brand, rather than necessarily the total strengths—and weaknesses—of the company as a whole. See Figure 9-7.

Campbell's CoreBrand Power has stayed strong even through multiple changes in management.

Familiarity and Favorability 1990 - 2001

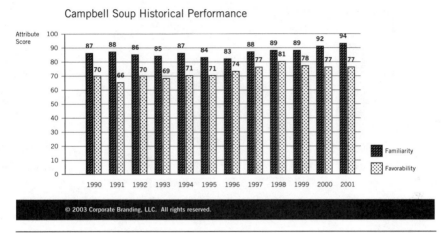

Campbell Soup Historical Performance

Figure 9-5. Familiarity and Favorability 1990–2001, Campbell Soup Historical Performance

CoreBrand Power 2001

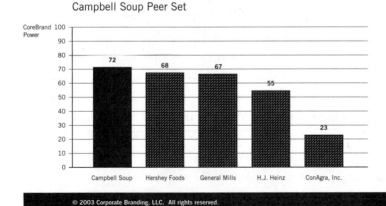

Campbell Soup Peer Set

Figure 9-6. CoreBrand Power 2001, Campbell Soup Peer Set

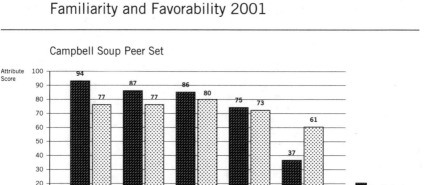

Familiarity and Favorability 2001

Campbell Soup Peer Set

Figure 9-7. Familiarity and Favorability 2001, Campbell Soup Peer Set

Faulkner says, "It's true that we had management turnover and reorganization. But in the last year we have announced our Transformation Plan for the future. Since then, perhaps the fact that Campbell has been a very profitable business for more than 130 years appears to be a little more attractive in the current marketplace."

But that doesn't mean everything is clear in the mind of the investment community. While Campbell's overall reputation has grown since 1999, its investment potential has eroded: See Figure 9-8.

"Has favorability towards our brand translated into investment activity?" Faulkner asks. "During the period where our reputation rebounded pretty dramatically, our stock price has declined. But we've also experienced a terrible bear market. You have to believe that over time, the underlying value of our brand will be recognized more fully by the investment community. But realistically, that will happen as our Transformation Plan gains traction in the marketplace."

The person chosen to lead the transition back to basics—and to profitability—was Douglas R. Conant, who was elected president and chief executive officer in January 2001.

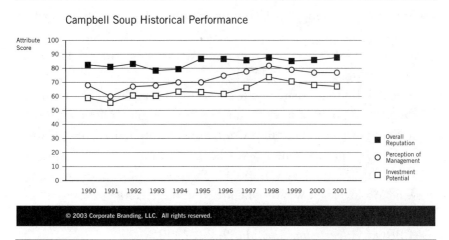

Figure 9-8. Favorability Attributes 1990–2001, Campbell Soup Historical Performance

"When our new CEO arrived, it was with the mandate from our Board to take a long-term look at our business," Faulkner says. "Doug was very clear with Wall Street when he unveiled our Transformation Plan. He said we would invest more in our marketing, to build our brands. And the company would invest in our infrastructure and in our people, as well. In the near term, that's going to impact the bottom line.

"But going forward, the intent is to deliver solid and predictable growth over the next 5 years," Faulkner continues. "Consistent growth, in the current investment climate, looks pretty attractive."

Notes

"Campbell Soup Label Gets a New Look after 100+ Years," News Releases, Financial Center, www.shareholder.com/campbells/news.

"Campbell Names Douglas R. Conant President and Chief Executive Officer," News Releases, Financial Center, www.shareholder.com/campbell/news, Jan. 8, 2001.

Campbell Soup Company, Annual Report 2000.

"Campbell's Looks to Old Slogan to Reheat Soup Sales," *The Food Institute Report*, Sept. 11, 2000.

Campbell Soup Company, Company Profile, Hoover's Online, www.hoovers.com.

"For the Record (Campbell Soup Co. Returns to Old Ad Theme)," *Advertising Age*, Sept. 11, 2000.

Interview: John Faulkner, Director, Corporate and Brand Communications, Campbell Soup Company, by Jim Gregory, March 8, 2002.

"The Story of Campbell Soup Company," Campbell History, Campbell's Community center, www.hoovers.com.

Jeff Fischer, "Canned by Campbell: Campbell Soup's CEO Resigns," The Motley Fool, www.fool.com, March 23, 2000.

Stephanie Thompson, "Campbell CEO Ouster Turns Up Heat on BBDO," *Advertising Age*, March 27, 2000.

Stephanie Thompson, "Campbell Cans Latest Soup Effort," *Advertising Age*, July 31, 2000.

Stephanie Thompson, "Campbell Fires Up Budget for Lines Other Than Soup," *Advertising Age*, March 12, 2001.

Stephanie Thompson, "Campbell Readies Ad Push to Revive Ailing V8 Splash," *Advertising Age*, Sept. 18, 2000.

Chapter Ten | **Best Practice No. 3**

Live the Brand

A couple of years ago, I mentioned Harley-Davidson in a speech to a group of CEOs in Bermuda, all insurance executives. This was about the stuffiest crowd you've ever seen in your life. Yet two of the CEOs came up to me separately afterwards; both of them rolled up their sleeves and showed me the Harley-Davidson logo tattooed on their biceps.

The Harley-Davidson brand has a power and mystique few corporations enjoy. Other motorcycle companies come and go, but H-D has a link with its audience that surpasses even the fine quality of its rides.

That's because the people at Harley-Davidson don't just make and sell the brand; they live it. They're riders and proud of it. Every year, hundreds of H-D employees spend time on the road, sharing the Harley-Davidson experience with their customers and prospects, meeting riders from all over the world . . . even going to rider weddings.

For decades, brand knowledge was transferred verbally, like tribal lore. H-D employees "get it" and are entrusted with major decisions; when they need help, H-D's Brand Council provides guidance on tough questions about everything from advertising to appropriate product licensing.

That cohesion shows in the steady rise of H-D's CoreBrand Power . . . not to mention all those new tattoos.

> *If you ride a Harley, you are a member of a brotherhood, and if you don't, you are not.*
>
> —Alec Wilkinson, *The New Yorker*

HARLEY-DAVIDSON
AN AMERICAN ICON, AN AMERICAN SUCCESS STORY

It isn't every brand that's an American icon . . . and even fewer that are true business success stories. Harley-Davidson epitomizes the best of both.

In 2003, Harley-Davidson celebrated its centennial. It all started back in 1903, when William Harley and the three Davidson brothers (Walter, William, and Arthur) began to sell a new contraption called a motorcycle. Not yet the famous Harley hog that we know today, riders had to pedal the original Harley-Davidson uphill. Even so, as production continued, demand was high enough that most of Harley-Davidson's motorcycles were sold before they ever left the factory.

Clearly, Harley and the Davidson brothers were on to something special. It wasn't long before they had over 150 competitors in the young motorcycle market, but Harley-Davidson maintained their leadership position through continuing innovation in engineering and design. Their trademark two-cylinder V-twin engine was introduced in 1909, and the teardrop gas tank in 1925.

World War I was a boom time for the motorcycle industry, as demand increased for lightweight, maneuverable transportation on the battlefields. But only a few years later, the Great Depression almost killed off the entire industry. Of the dozens of companies that had sprung up in the early part of the century, only two remained: Harley-Davidson and Indian. Global conflict once again helped boost the industry's fortunes during World War II, but by the early 1950s, even Indian was no more (although it has recently been revived).

In the 1960s and 1970s, competition heated up from overseas as British and Japanese manufacturers began to enter the U.S. market. Japanese bikes, in particular, were known for reliability and low prices. Unused to serious competition, H-D made a series of missteps that nearly resulted in the death of the brand.

In an attempt to diversify, the company began and later discontinued making a line of golf carts. In order to raise cash, Harley-Davidson went public in 1965. Four years later, it was sold to American Machine and Foundry (AMF). AMF tried to counter the onslaught of imported bikes by raising production levels, but higher production resulted in a loss of quality.

When sales continued to decline in favor of Japanese imports, AMF added its own name to the legendary H-D brand. With the dilution of the famous company name, sales plunged. Finally, AMF put the company up for sale again, but its prospects were so dismal that no buyer came forward. At last, a group of executives from Harley-Davidson wound up buying the company away from their former employer.

The new management brought back the Harley-Davidson name, but they still faced the key problem AMF had encountered, principally the sales being lost to a host of Japanese competitors. In addition, they were now trying to pay back $70 million in debt—during a recession and gasoline shortage. By 1983, the venerable Harley-Davidson was on the verge of bankruptcy.

Help came in the unlikely form of government intervention. Harley-Davidson executives lobbied hard for new federal tariffs on imports; the resulting tax helped stem the flow of foreign competition. In an ironic twist, H-D adopted the then-popular strategy of using Japanese management techniques to modernize their manufacturing process, expand their model lines, and improve quality across the board.

Eventually, Harley-Davidson executives were able to admit that the company's problems had less to do with their Japanese competition—and much more to do with their own internal issues. In an unprecedented move, H-D petitioned the International Trade Commission (ITC) in 1987 to lift the tariffs 1 year early. In an interview with the *New York Times*, then-CEO Vaughn Beals acknowledged that "we realized the problem was us."

But if "us" was the problem, it was also the solution. Despite all the miscues of the past years, H-D's biggest asset was still its brand. It's evoked in the distinctive sound of the V-twin engine (compared by one reporter to the sound of a T. rex with indigestion), the sight of a 665-pound Fat Boy with the distinctive teardrop gas tank, and the company's bar and shield logo.

But more than that, the Harley-Davidson brand is an attitude, a lifestyle, and in many cases, body art. William Blair & Co. analyst Richard Fradin told the *Chicago Tribune* that H-D "has the only brand that customers regularly tattoo on their bodies."

H-D's former chairman, Richard F. Teerlink, once observed that "Most people can't understand what would drive someone to profess his or her loyalty for our brand by tattooing our logo onto his or her body."

That's because owning a Harley is not just about owning a great bike: It's about having an adventurous attitude toward life.

More than 650,000 H-D owners around the world belong to H.O.G. (Harley Owners Group) chapters—and pay for the privilege of membership. They proudly go to rallies, Bike Weeks, and other events, mingling with other owners as well as H-D employees.

As a group these are consumers that other brands covet: The average H-D owner is in his mid-forties and earns more than $75,000 a year. And while some are still Hell's Angels (or dress like them), there are many more who are business men and women, preppies, grandparents, and what the industry calls "rubs"—rich urban bikers. Many H-D enthusiasts take their children or grandchildren along on road trips and rallies, introducing the next generation to Harley from the very beginning of their lives.

Research shows that almost 11 million people are interested in buying a Harley-Davidson bike. Buyers are so eager to own a Harley that they will wait for more than a year for delivery, once they've ordered a model from their dealer.

And their passion for H-D extends far beyond the ride: In March of 2002, Stacy Ann Gould and Jeff McAvoy became the first couple to be married in the world's first dealer-operated Harley-Davidson wedding chapel, arriving on their bikes and exchanging rings engraved with the H-D shield. Jeff Bleustein, Harley-Davidson Chairman and CEO, was among the guests.

Joanne Bischmann, H-D's Vice President of Marketing, says, "The Harley-Davidson brand is a little rebellious. We don't really like confinement; we're much more into freedom and doing things your own way. Our mission statement is, we fulfill dreams." You can see what they mean in the ad pictured in Figure 10-1.

Those dreams have fueled the renaissance of Harley-Davidson. Between 1985 and 2001, the company posted 17 consecutive years of record revenue and earnings.

Joanne Bischmann told us that while "there is no magic handbook, the growth that we've seen, first and foremost, is because we really know what the brand is, and we know what the brand is not."

For years, this brand knowledge was transmitted through what Bischmann calls "tribal knowledge." For almost a century, as employees joined H-D, they would observe, listen, and learn the culture and traditions inherent to the brand.

Bischmann equates the process to marrying into a family. "Just like when you get married, you might learn from a sister-in-law, for instance, that you shouldn't ever invite Jim and Judy to the same party; you learn to represent that family appropriately. That's kind of how it was with Harley-Davidson. We have policies, procedures, and programs, and all that, but mostly people would come in and observe, and they'd learn through tribal knowledge."

But that form of brand stewardship was to take a giant leap forward in 1996. Challenged by Jeff Bleustein to look beyond its twentieth-century parameters, the company developed its first formal brand identity model.

The new model helped the company define, clarify, and unify its brand platform in the United States as well as Europe and Asia.

Figure 10-1. Beginning in 2000, Harley-Davidson began focusing more on lifestyle. Even though their customers are (usually) law-abiding citizens, riding a Harley shows off their wild side. After all, as this ad says, "Lucky thing there's no law against having a little fun." (Photograph ©2003 Chris Wimpey; ad courtesy Harley-Davidson, Inc.)

As Joanne Bischmann recalls, "We got the whole company rally-
ing around one brand identity. Because the people who work on our
line, or in finance, or in customer service need to understand the
brand. That's where our strength comes from: Everybody is so consistent in their interaction and their communication of the brand."

The new brand model also helped the company look more closely
at its licensing arrangements. The H-D logo is on thousands of products, from personal care to clothing, from kids' toys to $5000 limited-
edition sculptures. In fact, H-D is one of the top five licensed brands
in the world. The model helped assure that licensing partners embodied the same innate irreverence as the Harley-Davidson brand, maintaining the brand's image with its passionate customers.

As Joanne Bischmann describes it, "We don't want to offend anybody, but we're more about the Tasmanian Devil than Mickey Mouse.
So if we looked at any type of animation house, for instance, we're
more in sync with Warner Brothers than we would be with Disney."

In 1997, through its new subsidiary, Eaglemark Financial Services, Inc., Harley expanded its empire—and customer relationships—
by introducing the Harley-Davidson Chrome VISA card. The card was
an instant hit among Harley enthusiasts, who used it to both finance
new bike purchases and to further their Harley lifestyle.

So what's Harley-Davidson's secret weapon?

Central to the company's brand program is its strategy of being
close to the customer. The H-D family of employees lives the brand as
fully (or almost—no one is required to sport a tattoo) as many of their
customers. Bischmann says, "They're the greatest marketing tool we
could possibly have."

For decades, H-D employees have mingled every year with H-D
riders at company-sponsored rallies. In 1998, 140,000 riders swarmed
Milwaukee to celebrate H-D's 95th anniversary. At these giant outdoor
events, people enjoy music, food, contests, and the chance to talk to
H-D staffers about their bikes. The 100th anniversary event, scheduled for August 2003, will include a parade of 10,000 bikes, as well as
three days of festivities. Tickets for the anniversary celebration—at
$55 each—were sold out weeks in advance.

According to Jeff Bleustein, "A lot of what you see in our product lines—and even the way we run our rallies—is the direct result of input we've received from our customers."

Willie G. (a/k/a William G. Davidson, H-D's Vice President of Styling and a grandson of one of the original Davidson brothers) put it bluntly. "We're riders," he said. "The best way for us to perpetuate the adventure is by living it and sharing it."

Employees are such a powerful part of H-D's marketing effort that the company does not even have a separate department focused on achieving brand objectives.

Joanne Bischmann says, "The one thing we did not want was a brand department. The goal is that everybody makes decisions in their own jobs; they're empowered to make the decisions."

Instead, the company created a Brand Council, whose role is to help staffers test tough decisions inside the company. The Brand Council is composed of seven managers from throughout the organization; each is senior in his or her department, but none is at the vice president level.

Originally Bischmann was going to rotate the Brand Council members every 2 years, but found that "Two years went very fast, considering we've had maybe four meetings in that amount of time. It's very rare that we'll have to call a Brand Council meeting. Which means that people do understand the brand identity and are making it work."

While Bischmann can call a meeting, she cannot vote on decisions that come up. A Brand Council meeting gets called when an employee has a difficult decision to make about whether a new idea will fit with the Harley-Davidson brand.

As Bischmann describes it, "They keep going up their chain of command and at some point, if they can't make the call or if they have enough concern over it, they'll call me and I'll call a Brand Council meeting."

The council members have a process to determine whether a particular product, product display, or other innovation is appropriate for the brand. The council does not give directives: Their role is to advise the employee on the impact his or her decision would have on the brand. The final decision about whether to proceed belongs to the employee.

According to Bischmann, "That's my best example of how we constantly practice empowerment. The whole brand identity process was built around something that people could use to make the decision themselves. So you're constantly watching that, you're training people, you're giving them the tools."

Like H-D's own employees, dealers are also encouraged to get closer to the customers and are given tools to help them do it. In recent years, dealerships have gone from being cycle shacks to full-fledged boutiques. In addition to moving Ultra Classic Electra Glide motorcycles at about $20,000 each, dealers sell that Harley feeling with leather jackets, chaps, jewelry, even baby clothes.

A new program encourages dealers to localize their showrooms, highlighting both the region and its biker culture. In Orlando, the Florida landscape inspired the colors and design of a new showroom, which was further embellished with black-and-white photos of real-life local bikers, and color photos of local roads and landmarks. The location, chosen for its proximity to both tourists and the local H.O.G. community, enjoyed quadrupled sales over the store's previous location and design.

The brand has solid numbers to back up its success. In 2000, Harley-Davidson was up to 56 percent of its market share. It produced 204,592 motorcycles, a 15.5 percent increase over the previous year. Between 1991 and 2000, Harley-Davidson's year-end stock price increased from $2.80 to $39.75.

During the past decade, Harley-Davidson's CoreBrand Power rating also experienced a huge increase, from 48 to 71. Although the brand's familiarity was high throughout that period, its favorability rating saw the most dramatic increase, signaling a shift in perception about H-D's management, stock, and overall reputation. Where growth had been solid in the first part of the 1990s, it took on an even more rapid pace after 1996, when the brand's image was clarified and solidified within the company. You can take a look at H-D's Core-Brand performance in Figures 10-2, 10-3, and 10-4.

CoreBrand Power 1990 - 2001

Harley-Davidson Historical Performance

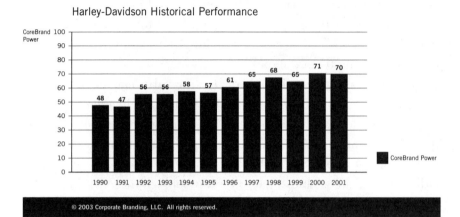

Figure 10-2. CoreBrand Power 1990–2001, Harley-Davidson Historical
Performance

Familiarity and Favorability 1990 - 2001

Harley-Davidson Historical Performance

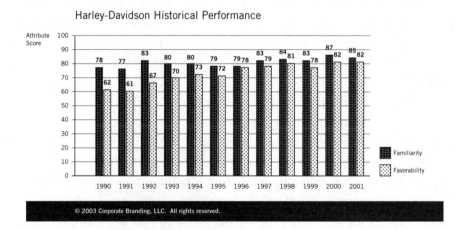

Figure 10-3. Familiarity and Favorability Attributes 1990–2001, Harley-
Davidson Historical Performance

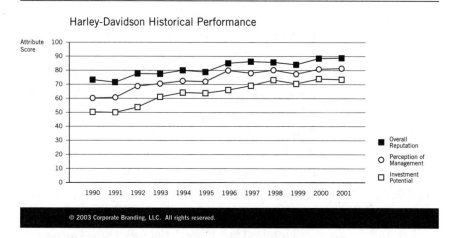

Figure 10-4. Favorability Attributes 1990–2001, Harley-Davidson Historical Performance

"I think really understanding the brand—always listening, talking, and communicating about the brand—has kept us in check, and, therefore, we know when we're doing the right things," Joanne Bischmann says. "Because when we're doing the wrong things, everybody lets us know—the analysts let us know, the dealers let us know, and most importantly, our customers let us know."

Notes

2002 Harley-Davidson Inc., Annual Report

"Experience Business," Harley-Davidson, Inc., 2000 Annual Report.

"Fitch Designs Orlando Harley-Davidson Store; Regional Branding Strategy Results in Quadrupled Sales," *Business Wire*, Feb. 27, 2001.

Harley-Davidson Background and History, Harley-Davidson Motor Company, 1999.

Harley-Davidson, Inc., Company Profile, Hoover's Online, www.hoovers.com.

Harley-Davidson, Licensed Brands, MDI Entertainment, www.
mdientertainment.com.

"Harley-Davidson: Marketing an American Icon," @ *Issue*, Corporate
Design Foundation, Volume 2, No. 1.

Interview with Joanne Bischmann, Harley-Davidson, by Jim Gregory,
Sept. 4, 2001.

"Ninety Years of Harley History," *Tulsa World*, Sept. 20, 2000.

"The Harley-Davidson Experience," 100th Anniversary FAQ, www.
harley-davidson.com

"Tickets on Sale for Harley-Davidson Milwaukee-Area 100th Anniversary Festivities," Harley-Davidson 100th Anniversary Media Site,
March 3, 2003, www.hdmedia.com.

"Timeline," 1990s, Harley-Davidson USA, www.harley-davidson.com

Kelly Barron, "Hog Wild. After Dominating the U.S. Motorcycle Market for 30 Years, Honda Has Fallen Behind Once-Struggling
Harley-Davidson. It Needs to Add a Little Torque to Its Marketing," *Forbes*, May 15, 2000, p. 68.

Mark Collins, "Hog Heaven," *Navigator*, Feb./March 2002.

Angela Daidone, "With Baby Boomers Fueling Growth, Harley-
Davidson Hogs the Motorcycle Market," *Knight-Ridder Tribune
Business News*, Sept. 24, 2000.

Ron Insana, "Interview: Jeffrey Bleustein, CEO of Harley-Davidson,
Discusses the Motorcycle Brand's Continued Popularity and
What's Coming Up for Their 100th Anniversary," CNBC Business
Center, June 12, 2001.

James P. Miller, "Hog Heaven/Harley-Davidson's Brand Strength
Makes It an Investor Darling, but Economic Flux May Cool Love
Affair," *Chicago Tribune*, Newsday, Inc., Jan. 28, 2001.

Glenn Rifkin, "How Harley-Davidson Revs Its Brand," *Strategy &
Business*, Fourth Quarter, 1997.

Jerry Shriver, "Richer, Older Harley Riders, 'Like Everyone Else,' "
USA Today, March 8–10, 2002.

Chapter Eleven | Best Practice No. 4

Create A Company Culture That Protects and Polishes Your Corporate Brand

Johnson & Johnson wants to make you and your family feel good. Perhaps best known for its signature line of baby care products, J&J makes a wide range of consumer goods as well as pharmaceuticals and professional healthcare products.

No matter where it does business, or what products it sells, Johnson & Johnson is known as a company you can trust. It hasn't gained this reputation by accident. J&J was founded on a commitment to improving healthcare, and it hasn't wavered from its dedication to make products that enhance and improve people's lives.

More than that, for 60 years, Johnson & Johnson has functioned according to a set of guidelines that outline the responsibilities of both the corporation and every single employee. Despite outside crises, changes in the market, and the growth of its business, adherence to these guidelines worldwide has kept J&J's reputation sky-high . . . and its CoreBrand Power towering over its competitors.

> *We guard the reputation of this company with our lives.*
> —Bill Nielsen, Vice President of Public Affairs,
> Johnson & Johnson

JOHNSON & JOHNSON
A MATTER OF TRUST

In February 2003, Harris Interactive and The Reputation Institute released the results of their latest survey, based on the responses of 26,000 consumers. For the fourth year in a row, Johnson & Johnson was found to have the best corporate reputation in America.

In fact, J&J's reputation is its most carefully regarded—and guarded—asset. Every aspect of the company is run according to principles laid down decades ago, in a remarkable document called the Credo.

The result is a company whose name evokes, in the words of Bill Nielsen, J&J Vice President of Public Affairs, "a sense of deep personal trust."

The company does not even think of its famous signature logo as a trademark; former Chairman and CEO Ralph S. Larsen called the Johnson & Johnson name "more than a trademark . . . it has become a 'trustmark' known in virtually every corner of the world."

Yet Johnson & Johnson is a massive global entity, with more than 200 operating companies in 54 countries. It produces a wide range of products, from baby care, skin care, first aid, contraceptive care, and contact lenses to hospital products, prescription pharmaceuticals, and diagnostic tools.

How does such a far-flung corporation, with thousands of products, maintain such a strong association with trust in the minds of consumers and opinion leaders?

According to Bill Nielsen, "We know that awareness of J&J is quite high; we also know that favorability is quite high. We also know that when you ask people why they feel so good about it, they can't describe it very accurately; it's a sort of a warm and fuzzy sense of caring and trust.

"And everybody says, well, if they can't define it, then that's a problem. But I think a lot of us who have studied this now for a while are not convinced that's a problem. We know that the attributes associated with it are very unique: We can't find another entity that evokes quite the same sentiment. So what we focus on is how we behave and what we say, so that we don't disturb the brand."

J&J's roots lie in one of the greatest discoveries in healthcare: the realization that germs cause disease—and even death.

Hard as it is to believe now, as recently as the nineteenth century surgeons used to operate wearing their everyday clothes. They worked barehanded, without gloves. Instruments were not sterilized, and surgical dressings were made from cotton swept up from the floors of textile mills. Despite infections that routinely killed up to 90 percent of post-op patients, doctors had a hard time believing that the problems were due to tiny, airborne, living organisms—germs—that thrived on their clothes, instruments, and surgical supplies.

But some people saw an opportunity to change the status quo. Sir Joseph Lister was the doctor who first identified germs as "invisible assassins." In 1876, a young man named Robert Wood Johnson attended one of his lectures. For years afterward, Johnson toyed with the idea of an improved surgical dressing, one that would be sterile, wrapped, and ready to use.

Robert's two brothers, James and Edward Mead, were already in the medical supply business: They opened the doors of their own company in 1885, in New Brunswick, New Jersey. Robert joined the partnership a year later, and the company was soon incorporated as Johnson & Johnson.

Not long afterward, the company introduced a cotton and gauze surgical dressing that could be shipped to hospitals, druggists, and doctors around the country. This was the first fruit of Robert's vision for improving healthcare for patients. Company scientists continued the search for a sterile dressing and went on to produce a number of advances, including sterilization techniques for both dressings and sutures.

J&J entered the consumer market with the introduction of Johnson's Baby Powder in 1893. From the beginning, the brand messages focused on doing what was best for baby—and for mom. Over the next century, J&J would become inextricably linked with baby care. J&J advertised heavily in this category throughout the twentieth century, contributing greatly to consumers' awareness and favorability toward the company . . . even though the vast majority of J&J's products are in other categories, and marketed under other names.

Robert's son, also called Robert Wood Johnson, eventually inherited the mantle of leadership for the company. The younger Robert had championed J&J's international expansion while still a young man, after a trip around the world. He also served as a brigadier general in World War II and forever after was known as the General.

The General took over as CEO in 1932; his imprint on the company was formidable. It was he who created the company's 308-word mission statement, known as the Credo. Those words are quite literally carved in stone at company headquarters, which are still in New Brunswick, New Jersey. The Credo is J&J's Ten Commandments and Bill of Rights rolled into one. It's printed in full in Figure 11-1. The Credo states the responsibilities of the company, and of each J&J employee, in order of importance:

- "We believe our first responsibility is to the doctors, nurses and patients, to mothers and fathers and all others who use our products and services . . .
- "Our suppliers and distributors must have an opportunity to make a fair profit . . .
- "We are responsible to our employees, the men and women who work with us throughout the world . . .
- "We are responsible to the communities in which we live and work and to the world community as well . . .
- "Our final responsibility is to our stockholders . . . [because] when we operate according to these principles, the stockholders should realize a fair return."

The Credo is at the heart of J&J's ability to maintain and even improve its reputation year after year. Protecting J&J's reputation is among its highest priorities. As Bill Nielsen told us, "we put an emphasis on behavior consistent with our Credo as the only way that perhaps we can enhance the standing of the corporation. We work

OUR CREDO

We believe our first responsibility is to the doctors, nurses and patients,
to mothers and fathers and all others who use our products and services.
In meeting their needs everything we do must be of high quality.
We must constantly strive to reduce our costs
in order to maintain reasonable prices.
Customers' orders must be serviced promptly and accurately.
Our suppliers and distributors must have an opportunity
to make a fair profit.

We are responsible to our employees,
the men and women who work with us throughout the world.
Everyone must be considered as an individual.
We must respect their dignity and recognize their merit.
They must have a sense of security in their jobs.
Compensation must be fair and adequate,
and working conditions clean, orderly and safe.
We must be mindful of ways to help our employees fulfill
their family responsibilities.
Employees must feel free to make suggestions and complaints.
There must be equal opportunity for employment, development
and advancement for those qualified.
We must provide competent management,
and their actions must be just and ethical.

We are responsible to the communities in which we live and work
and to the world community as well.
We must be good citizens — support good works and charities
and bear our fair share of taxes.
We must encourage civic improvements and better health and education.
We must maintain in good order
the property we are privileged to use,
protecting the environment and natural resources.

Our final responsibility is to our stockholders.
Business must make a sound profit.
We must experiment with new ideas.
Research must be carried on, innovative programs developed
and mistakes paid for.
New equipment must be purchased, new facilities provided
and new products launched.
Reserves must be created to provide for adverse times.
When we operate according to these principles,
the stockholders should realize a fair return.

Johnson&Johnson

Figure 11-1. J&J Credo. General Robert Wood Johnson wrote the Johnson & Johnson Credo in 1943. Today, it is engraved in stone at company headquarters. (Source: Johnson & Johnson.)

on our behaviors to make sure we don't step out of line. And we engage in activities that people would perceive as the act of a trust-worthy company, and does what they would expect from Johnson & Johnson."

The Credo is also how J&J maintains another of General Johnson's key principles: decentralization. As the company grew, an ever-increasing number of divisions and affiliates were given the autonomy to manage their own businesses—without interference from senior management.

Decentralization also allows the company to operate in a culture of trust: Employees are given the freedom to succeed, as well as fail. Former CEO Ralph S. Larsen observed, "The quickest way to destroy morale is to issue edicts from New Brunswick." In fact, Larsen noted, J&J's managers virtually always "come up with better solutions and set tougher standards for themselves than I would have imposed."

One result is that J&J is consistently rated as one of the best work-places in the country, by the Harris Survey and others. In turn, J&J's employees are fiercely loyal to the brand. While the overall responsi-bility for preserving and maintaining the brand image belongs to the CEO, managers at every level work to protect the brand and its image of trust.

Dan Laughhunn, a professor at Duke University's School of Busi-ness, told *Fortune* that J&J "is a company of worriers. They're very self-critical. No matter how good they are, they look where they are weak."

Bill Nielsen sheds more light on how seriously J&J staff take their responsibilities: "The slightest thing that comes along, we're terrified that it's going to tarnish the name, and it's going to be on our watch, but it doesn't happen."

He continues, "I'm very leery of any suggestion that we can man-age the brand. I think what we do around here is we pay a lot of respect to it and we try not to use it, and we certainly don't allow it to be used. You have to go through considerable hoops around here to associate the corporate name with any product or service. It requires a specific sign-off by the CEO."

Of course, J&J can and does manage its brand. The most famous—and extreme—example is the Tylenol crisis of 1982. The company's management of that disaster—in which bottles of Tylenol were tampered with and laced with cyanide, eventually killing eight people—not only reinforced the public's trust, but saved the Tylenol brand.

Nielsen says that, as a rule, "You can't go back and say 'trust us.' That was done one time, at high risk following the Tylenol poisoning in '82. But what you can do is be seen by your public to be engaged in the acts of a trustworthy company."

That's why J&J's version of corporate advertising does not actually tout the company's many products. Nielsen explains, "We have struggled for a long time with the issue of a 'corporate campaign.' We don't generally do corporate advertising just to tout the company— we're out there addressing an issue or concern in society. It goes back to the question that if people have a sense of deep, personal trust in Johnson & Johnson, how do you enhance that?"

In 1999, J&J ran a campaign called "How to Talk to Your Kids." Starring Ray Romano, Christopher Reeve, Randy Newman, and Toni Morrison, the series of commercials offered practical tips on how parents can improve communications with their children. A sample frame from a spot starring Ray Romano is shown in Figure 11-2.

Nielsen remembers that the campaign "was already in the works at about the time of the Columbine situation, and we actually waited a while to release it because we didn't want it to be perceived as our answer to that issue. But it was pretty well received. And again, it was the kind of thing that only Johnson & Johnson could do."

In 2001, J&J launched a campaign focusing on the shortage of nurses in the United States. Nielsen says that one reason J&J got behind the issue "is because healthcare providers are our customers and they have a huge problem: They can't provide the level of care that they want because of the nursing shortage. So there's sort of an enlightened self-interest in taking up the cause."

The campaign met with great acclaim, not least from the American Nursing Association. Nielsen says the campaign is "about the

Figure 11-2. Campaign frame: Comedian Ray Romano talked about the importance of laughter in J&J's "How to Talk to Kids" campaign. (Source: Johnson & Johnson.)

future of nursing. We're trying to improve the image of nurses. The program has a Web site and scholarships—it's really just sweeping the country."

J&J's next corporate campaign will touch back on its most famous consumer franchise: baby care. But true to form, the campaign won't be about J&J products. Nielsen says the plan is to develop "some very subtle but firm reinforcement of the imagery around infant care, and associating those images with Johnson & Johnson."

Clearly, the value of J&J's reputation is seen in its CoreBrand Power, which towers over its nearest peer, Procter & Gamble.

The company's favorability rating dipped twice in the 1990s, once between 1992 and 1994, with a smaller decline between 1998 and 1999. In the mid-1990s, all three factors affecting J&J's favorability declined together; the perception of the company's investment potential stayed down the longest. Bill Nielsen says that the downward trend was due to concerns about the proposed Clinton healthcare reform.

In 1999, the decline in favorability was both less steep and shorter-lived. This time the problem was with issues more directly related to the company: Several drugs in development did not get to market, and the company lost its leading position in the market for coronary artery stents.

Since 1999, however, the company's favorability rating has been consistently rising upward . . . and bringing its CoreBrand Power up with it, from 69 in 1999 to 74 in 2001. You can see J&J's CoreBrand Power history in Figures 11-3, 11-4, and 11-5.

In their 2002 Letter to Shareholders, Chairman and CEO William C. Weldon, and Vice Chairman and President James T. Lenehan sum up the strategy that has driven the organization's extraordinary performance for so many years. They wrote: "We pursue [our] growth by managing against a set of broad principles: maintaining a broadly based healthcare business, stressing a decentralized system of management, and managing for the long term on a foundation of values as espoused in Our Credo."

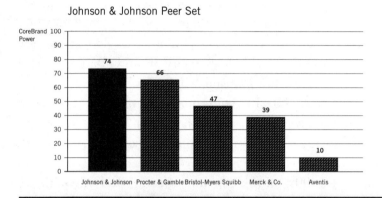

Figure 11-3. CoreBrand Power 2001, Johnson & Johnson Peer Set

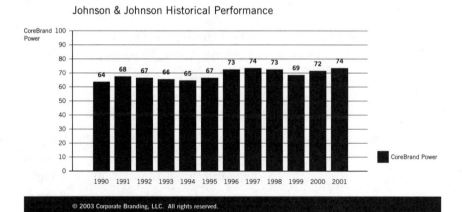

Figure 11-4. CoreBrand Power 1990–2001, Johnson & Johnson Historical Performance

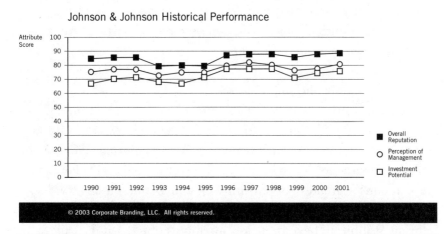

Figure 11-5. Favorability Attributes 1990–2001, Johnson & Johnson Historical Performance

Nielsen points out, "If you look at the numbers, the performance in this company, it's a hundred years of a steady line going up and that's what we're going to protect." J&J has never lost money since it went public in 1944—earning the trust of its shareholders as well as its customers.

Nielsen also offers some insights about how J&J's CoreBrand Power strengthens its business proposition globally.

"First of all," he explains, "the reputation is exceptionally strong, and it's exceptionally resilient compared to other multinational businesses.

"Secondly," he continues, "the strength of the reputation, and the awareness and recognition of the corporate name in the United States, is a key element to Johnson & Johnson's standing globally, particularly among influentials and opinion leaders in countries all over the world, even though we don't have the same kind of recognition among the general public in those countries. We know that it makes a difference, for instance, if we're trying to get a new drug on the market, so if our reputation and standing in the United States suffered it would hurt us around the world. That's an article of faith.

"The third point is that the attributes of trust and caring that are most frequently associated with Johnson & Johnson are also unique among major multinationals. You don't see those words together very often when you mention a big name.

"And as a result of all of this we do regard the brand as an extremely valuable and unique asset."

J&J will continue to protect its brand, carefully maintaining and improving its reputation over time. It continues to expand into new areas, from skin care to biotechnology. While pointing out that the company always needs "to be very, very careful," Nielsen believes that the company's greatest opportunity lies in maintaining awareness, reinforcing imagery associated with the brand, but never "defining" Johnson & Johnson beyond its key attributes of trust and caring.

"I think people form multiple views of the company," Nielsen says. "Great stock, impressive pharmaceutical company, caring company. Okay to get next to my baby."

Notes

"Balancing Work & Family," Johnson & Johnson, www.johnsonand johnson.com.

"Company History," Johnson & Johnson, www.johnsonandjohnson. com.

"Credo," Johnson & Johnson, www.johnsonandjohnson.com.

Interview, Bill Nielsen, Vice President of Public Affairs, Johnson & Johnson, by Jim Gregory, March 5, 2002.

"Johnson & Johnson," Company Capsule, Hoovers Online, www. hoovers.com.

Johnson & Johnson 2002 Historical Financial Review.

"Johnson & Johnson Launches New Ad Campaign," www.jnj.com/ news, Dec. 10, 1999.

Dean Boyer, "Johnson's Baby Products," Personal Products, *Encyclopedia of Consumer Brands*, Vol. II.

Ralph S. Larsen, et al., "Letter to Shareowners," March 14, 2001.

Brian O'Reilly, "J&J Is on a Roll," *Fortune*, Dec. 16, 1994.

Carol Stavraka, "Strong Corporate Reputation at J&J Boosts Diversity Recruiting Efforts," Diversity Workforce, DiversityInc.com, www.diversityinc.com.

William C. Weldon and James T. Lenehan, Letter to Shareholders, Johnson & Johnson 2002 Annual Report.

Chapter Twelve

Best Practice No. 5

Align Your Brand with Your Business

When Philip Morris Companies, Inc., asked its shareholders to consider a new name for the holding company giant, then-CEO Geoffrey C. Bible wrote a memo to employees explaining the reasons for the change.

"So, why are we proposing this?" the memo asked. "And why now?"

The first reason, Bible wrote, was "the need for clarity . . . A new name for the corporate parent will clarify our corporate identity."

The second reason, Bible wrote, was "our business evolution. We are not the same family of companies we were when Philip Morris Companies, Inc., was established."

Bible and his management team realized that with the growth of Philip Morris and its expansion into consumer products, its famous—and controversial—identity no longer matched its operating companies' portfolio of products and services.

It was time to reevaluate the corporate brand.

> *Even among opinion elites, people think Philip Morris is either just*
> *a tobacco company, or a tobacco company that owns a food com-*
> *pany—neither of which is true.*
>
> —Steven Parrish,
> Senior Vice President of Corporate Affairs,
> Altria Group, Inc.

PHILIP MORRIS COMPANIES—ALTRIA
A HISTORIC BRAND CREATES A NEW IDENTITY

Say the name "Philip Morris" to someone and you're bound to get an opinion . . . if not start an argument. As the top seller of the world's largest brands of cigarettes, Philip Morris has spent more than a decade under fire for its core business: selling tobacco.

By 2001, Philip Morris Companies, Inc., (PMC) was not only one of the world's top cigarette producers and the maker of Marlboro, the leading worldwide brand, it had become the largest consumer pack-aged-goods company in the world, with names like Kraft Foods and Miller Brewing in its portfolio.

Even so, the company remained famous for tobacco. While the company had fended off antismoking activists for over a century, its reputation—and stock price—gradually fell to the rising tide of the antismoking sentiment of the 1990s. By 1999, *BusinessWeek* was calling PMC "America's most reviled company."

The company had to do something to protect its brand and its survival. The change proved to be dramatic.

It all started simply enough. In 1847, a gentleman named Philip Morris opened his own tobacconist store in London's Old Bond Street. His timing was good: English boys returning from the brutal Crimean war came home with a newly acquired taste for Turkish cigarettes. Under their influence, cigarette smoking—once a habit only of the poor—became fashionable. Within a few years, Morris was producing his own blend of hand-rolled Turkish cigarettes, and the small busi-ness prospered.

After Mr. Morris passed away in 1873, his name—and business—survived, remaining a valuable asset for a series of new owners. The brand gained additional cachet in 1901 when Philip Morris & Co., Ltd., was appointed tobacconist for King Edward VII. When Edward abdicated to marry Wallis Simpson, his successor, King Albert, renewed the appointment.

In 1902, Philip Morris & Co. came to the New World, setting up shop on Broad Street in downtown New York City. It carved out a niche selling its British brands, including Cambridge, Oxford Blues, English Ovals, Players, and one named Marlborough.

Marlboro—with its new "American" spelling—was marketed in the 1920s as a woman's cigarette that was "Mild as May." Marlboro targeted "decent, respectable" women, who "quickly develop discerning taste. That is why Marlboros now ride in so many limousines, attend so many bridge parties, and repose in so many handbags."

In 1954, in a bold move to grow the brand, ad agency Leo Burnett created the Marlboro Cowboy. The slogan was "Delivers the Goods on Flavor." At the time, Marlboro had one-quarter of 1 percent of the American market. Ten years later, the Cowboy became the star of his own campaign, "Marlboro Country." The new slogan was "Come to where the flavor is. Come to Marlboro Country." Marlboro sales began growing 10 percent each year. (In 1999 *Ad Age* would dub "Marlboro Country" the Number 3 ad campaign of the century.) In time, Marlboro would become the biggest-selling brand-name cigarette in the world.

But, perhaps inevitably, during the years of Marlboro's—and Philip Morris Companies'—most dramatic growth, the pace of government regulation—and consumer antismoking activism—began to increase.

A major turning point occurred on a quiet Saturday morning in 1964. At 7:30 AM, two copies of a 387-page, brown-covered document were hand-delivered to the West Wing of the White House. Ninety minutes later, waiting reporters were admitted to a secure auditorium in the State Department, where they were locked inside the room, with no access to phones, and given 90 minutes to review Surgeon General Luther L. Terry, M.D.'s Report on Smoking and Health.

The story that flashed out at 10:30 AM became one of the top news items of 1964: It was the first time that the American government officially recognized cigarette smoking as a cause of cancer and other serious diseases. But it wouldn't be the last. In 1965, Congress passed the Federal Cigarette Labeling Act, requiring cigarette companies to put a prominent warning label on all cigarette packages. In 1971, cigarette advertising was banned on radio and television. The following year, health warnings were required on all advertising, direct mail, and point-of-sale materials.

Between 1967 and 2001, the surgeon general issued 26 more reports on the hazards of smoking, with such titles as "The Health Consequences of Smoking," "Preventing Tobacco Use Among Young People," and "Women and Smoking."

Consumers began demanding smoke-free environments. In 1970, TWA began to offer no-smoking sections aboard every flight. By 1973, the Civil Aeronautics Board had mandated nonsmoking sections for all airlines. By 1990, all domestic U.S. flights of less than 6 hours were completely smoke-free.

Other venues followed. In 1993, President Clinton banned smoking in the White House. In 1994, OSHA (Occupational Safety and Health Administration) proposed severe workplace smoking restrictions. The Department of Defense restricted smoking at all U.S. military bases worldwide. Even McDonald's banned smoking in all of its 11,000 restaurants.

As the social climate changed, litigation increased. In 1994, Mississippi became the first state to sue tobacco companies to recover healthcare costs associated with smoking. Three years later, the tobacco companies settled the case for $3.6 billion. In the meantime, other states took up the offense, eventually winning multimillion-dollar and billion-dollar awards against Philip Morris as well as competitors R.J. Reynolds, Liggett, American Tobacco, and others.

In 1996, the first class-action lawsuit against tobacco companies was allowed to proceed to trial. The plaintiffs in the Engle trial included all Florida residents or their survivors, who suffered from diseases caused by nicotine. The jury ruled that smoking causes diseases such as lung cancer, and that U.S. cigarette makers had hidden the dangers of their products from the public. Four years later, the plaintiffs were awarded $12.7 million in damages, and a staggering $145 billion in punitive damages. The shockwaves to the industry were enormous. (Three years after the judgment, in May 2003, a Florida appeals court reversed the ruling, denying the legality of class action lawsuits against the tobacco industry. The court did uphold the right of individuals to file suits against tobacco companies.)

Not coincidentally, 1996 was the first year that Philip Morris Companies' CoreBrand Power rating took a serious dive, plunging from 52 in 1995 to 38 in 1996, driven largely by decreased favorability. You can see the changes the company experienced throughout the 1990s in Figures 12-1, 12-2, and 12-3.

Steven Parrish, Altria's Senior Vice President of Corporate Affairs, compares working at Philip Morris in the mid-1990s to living in a bunker. PM employees felt unprepared to handle attacks from the

Figure 12-1. CoreBrand Power 1990–2001, Philip Morris Companies, Inc., Historical Performance

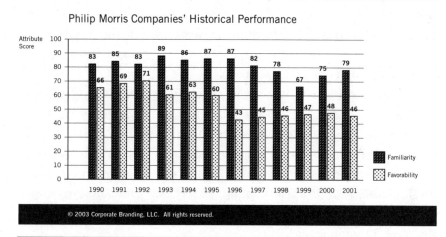

Figure 12-2. Familiarity and Favorability 1990–2001, Philip Morris Companies, Inc., Historical Performance

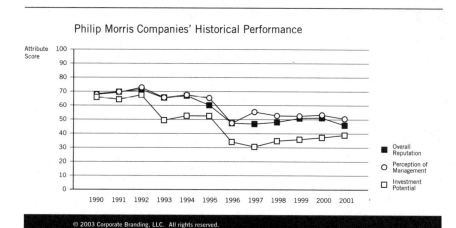

Figure 12-3. Favorability Attributes 1990–2001, Philip Morris Companies, Inc., Historical Performance

media, the government, and even their friends, who were known to ask, "How can you work for a company that kills people?"

Perception of management had dropped like a stone. Geoffrey Bible, CEO from 1994 to 2002, realized that the company had to step up and demonstrate its commitment to work with the government, the courts, and consumers. In the words of Steven Parrish, "we need[ed] to align ourselves with society."

Eventually this new attitude helped lead to the historic 1998 settlement between the U.S. tobacco industry and the attorneys general of 46 states. The tobacco companies agreed to ban cigarette ads targeting young people, and to pay out approximately $206 billion over 25 years to cover costs of Medicaid and other tobacco-related claims and lawsuits. In return, the companies received protection from further state suits. For Philip Morris, the price tag of the settlement was about $4.5 billion a year.

The federal government used the 1998 agreement to leverage its own case against Big Tobacco. In his January 1999 State of the Union address, President Clinton asked Congress "to resist the tobacco lobby, to reaffirm the FDA's authority to protect our children from tobacco and to hold tobacco companies accountable . . . So tonight I announce that the Justice Department is preparing a litigation plan to take the tobacco companies to court and with the funds we recover to strengthen Medicare."

The Justice Department filed its complaint the following September in U.S. District Court in Washington. The defendants included Philip Morris as well as R.J. Reynolds, Brown & Williamson, Lorillard, British American Tobacco, and The Council for Tobacco Research. The complaint accused cigarette makers of a "coordinated campaign of fraud and deceit" and even included two counts of violating the RICO Statute (Racketeer Influenced Corrupt Organizations).

Individuals also pressed successful suits, many specifically against Philip Morris USA, PMC's domestic tobacco company. Juries awarded huge amounts of money for medical costs, pain, and suffering . . . and, as in Engle, even higher amounts in punitive damages. In 1999, Californian Patricia Henley won $1.5 million from Philip Morris for medical costs, pain, and suffering . . . and $51.5 million in punitive damages (the award was later reduced to $26.5 million). In Oregon, the family of Jesse Williams received about $800,000 in compensatory damages and $79.5 million in punitive damages. (As of this writing, the state courts have upheld these two awards.)

In the midst of this turmoil, the company began to add to its already diverse holdings, hedging its bets against the possibility that they might be regulated—or sued—out of the tobacco business. Back in 1970, Philip Morris had acquired Miller Brewing. In the 1980s, under CEO Hamish Maxwell, PMC acquired General Foods and then Kraft, each in turn the largest non-oil acquisition in U.S. history. The two companies were combined to become Kraft Foods, Inc. (PMC later consolidated its food holdings by acquiring Nabisco in 2000, creating the world's second-largest food company after Nestlé S.A.)

In the 1990s, the company focused strongly on international expansion, acquiring Jacobs-Suchard AG, a Swiss coffee and confectionery company, as well as other firms in Scandinavia, the United Kingdom, Brazil, Eastern Europe, and the former Soviet Union. By 1995, international revenues ($32 billion) exceeded domestic for the first time ($31.4 billion), even as domestic profits and market share continued to grow every year.

But record profits at home and abroad didn't assuage investor fears about the onslaught of lawsuits and the enormous sums being awarded to plaintiffs. In 1999, hurt by Engle and other judgments, Philip Morris Companies' stock slid 50 percent, losing $83.2 billion in stock market value. In Geoffrey Bible's words, the company was "the dog of the Dow."

That year, PMC was as low as it had ever been. *BusinessWeek* declared, "Rarely has an industry or a corporation been so deeply vilified and so thoroughly discredited as Big Tobacco and its biggest player, Philip Morris." PMC's CoreBrand Power had fallen to 31, an all-time low, in large part due to its fallen investment potential.

But 1999 was also when Philip Morris Companies decided to change course. As Steven Parrish recalls, that was the year PMC came out of the bunker: In October, the company introduced a new corporate campaign to rehabilitate its image, with the theme, "Working to make a difference. The people of Philip Morris."

As Steven Parrish told us, "When we launched our campaign, the employees—and not just the tobacco employees, but people across the enterprise—were extraordinarily happy that we were finally speaking out. So that was great; they loved the commercials. They loved the fact that we were out making speeches around the country. And we got a lot of the employees involved in making those speeches, from all levels of the company, from all parts of the business, just talking about the company."

But Philip Morris Companies had made a commitment not just to meet the letter of the law but also to match its spirit.

"For a long time," Parrish says, "I think the culture here was, let's do everything we can to make sure we're obeying the law, and that we are not violating any laws. Then we started talking about societal alignment—making sure that we either meet or exceed society's expectations of us as a business. I think now people see the culture is much more than just compliance—it's integrity, it's responsibility—and they feel good about that."

By 2001, PMC's operating companies had nearly 12 $1 billion-per-year brands, including Marlboro, Maxwell House, Post, Miller, Kraft, Nabisco, and Oscar Mayer. It had become the world's largest and most profitable consumer packaged-goods company, although tobacco remained two-thirds of the business.

After leading the company through most of the tumultuous 1990s, then-CEO Bible publicly redefined the company. In a March 2001 speech, Bible said, "Philip Morris Companies defines itself not as a tobacco company, but as a consumer products company, with a particular expertise in products intended for adult consumers."

The leadership of Philip Morris Companies had come face to face with two diverging realities. As Philip Morris Companies, Inc., the holding company encompassed far more than tobacco. However, as long as the parent company shared the name of the tobacco units (Philip Morris USA and Philip Morris International), the social, financial, and legal pressures on cigarette makers would continue to affect perceptions of not just the Philip Morris tobacco brands but the rest of the company as well. The company known as "Philip Morris" was about a lot more than cigarettes, but, apparently, nobody knew it.

It was time for the company to align its identity with its new reality, both internally and externally.

The company scheduled a presentation to announce that they were considering a name change for the holding company. The meeting was to take place at New York's Hyatt Hotel on September 17, 2001.

The Tuesday before, however, was September 11. Philip Morris Companies canceled the conference, pulled its advertising, and redirected its communications budget to relief efforts.

In November, the company publicly asked its shareholders to approve the parent company's proposed name change, from Philip Morris Companies, Inc., to Altria Group, Inc. You can see the ad they created in Figure 12-4.

The new name, derived from the Latin word *altus*, for high, was meant to signify *peak performance*, as well as the company's aspirations to continue reaching ever higher. The shareholders' meeting to ratify the change took place in April 2002 and was approved with more than 95 percent of the votes cast.

Speaking of his planned speech for the original meeting, Steven Parrish says, "I was going to say that our research has shown us that, despite the fact that our favorability has improved, people are still confused about the company. Even among opinion elites, overwhelmingly people think 'Philip Morris' is either just a tobacco company, or a tobacco company that owns a food company—neither of which is true. They don't understand we're this parent company with food, beer, and tobacco.

"And as long as people think we're a tobacco company," Parrish continues, "there is going to be a wall that we're going to hit with a portion of the people we're trying to improve our image with."

While there were two lawsuits brought by smaller companies over the Altria name, the change met with a relatively positive reaction.

Parrish says, "Actually, we were sort of pleasantly surprised that

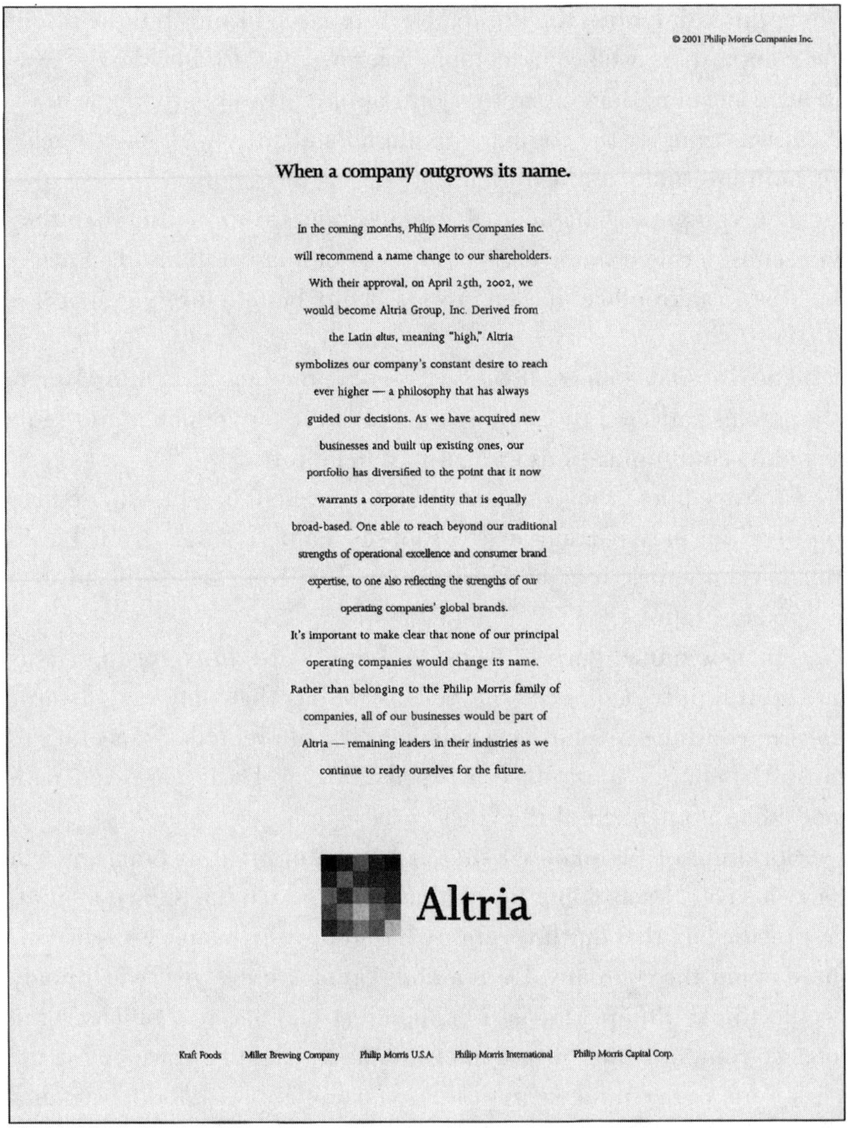

Figure 12-4. Altria ad, announcing its proposed name change.

there wasn't as much negative reaction as we thought we'd get. We were prepared for the employees to say, 'We don't like this. You're giving in to the people who are trying to destroy us. You're walking away from the tobacco business.'

"And we were prepared for everybody to say, 'What a stupid name.' Landor, our naming consultants, told us that anytime you change the name, particularly if you change to a coined name, people initially won't like it.

"And that turned out to be pretty much true. The employees understood the rationale for changing the name, they were fine with changing the name, and then they were about 50/50 on the particular name that we were proposing."

What does it mean to change the name of a brand after more than a century of success?

Parrish says, "Somebody asked me what my definition of a short-term success would be on the name change. Here's what I said to them: First of all, my definition of short term is 12 to 18 months. We can identify three key audiences for our name change and the identity: employees, investors, and opinion leaders. The brand building, the relationship building for the general public should come from our operating companies, because they're the ones who sell the products to members of the general public.

"So at the end of the short term," Parrish continues, "I would like those three target audiences to understand why we changed the name, to agree that it was a good idea to change the name, and that we did it well. I don't care at the end of 12 to 18 months whether they like the name. I'll worry about that after I convince them that it made sense to change the name and they understand why we felt the need to change the name."

Now the business known as Philip Morris has returned to its roots as a tobacco company. As Michael Buettner reported for the Associated Press, "The Philip Morris name—solidified with the public through the longtime radio advertising slogan "Call for Philip Morris"—will survive only in the company's tobacco operating divisions and in the stock symbol, which will remain MO."

Parrish says the message Philip Morris has to communicate is
"'Yes, we are in the tobacco business.' Understand that's, to put it
mildly, controversial for a lot of people, but let us tell you some of the
things that we're doing to try to be responsible in this very controversial business."

Investors have given Altria an initial thumbs-up. The parent company's stock price has regained much of its lost value, and its Core-
Brand Power has improved slightly, although it hasn't achieved its
pre-litigation levels of the early 1990s.

As for whether Altria will achieve success as a corporate brand,
which its name clearly strives for, we think its chances—like its aspirations—are high.

Notes

1999 State of the Union Address, Federal News Service, Jan. 20, 1999,
    http://www.washingtonpost.com/wp-srv/politics/special/states/
    docs/sou99.htm#tobacco.

"At a Glance," Nestlé USA, http://www.nestleusa.com/corporate
    Site/ataglance/at_a_glance.asp.

"California Appellate Court Reaffirms Henley Verdict: Philip Morris
    USA Will Appeal," Altria, Media, Press Release, March 20, 2003.

Company & Products, Philip Morris USA, http://www.philipmorris
    usa.com.

Conference Call Transcript, Nick Rolli: Moderator, announcing Altria
    name to analysts, Nov. 16, 2001.

"Florida Appeals Court Reverses Engle Judgment; Unanimous Panel
    Orders Class Decertified," Altria Press Release, May 21, 2003.

Historical Fact Sheet, Tobacco Information and Prevention Source,
    National Center for Chronic Disease Prevention and Health
    Promotion; http://www.cdc.gov/tobacco/sgr/sgr_2000/factsheets/
    factsheet_historical.htm.

History of the 1964 Surgeon General's Report on Smoking and
    Health, 1964 Surgeon General's Report on Smoking and Health,
    www.cdc.gov/tobacco/30yrsgen.htm.

History of Tobacco, Brown & Williamson Tobacco, http://www.bw.
    com/index_sub2.cfm?Page=/BWT/Index.cfm%3FID%3D99%
    26Sect%3D4.

Interview: Steven C. Parrish, Senior Vice President of Corporate
    Affairs, Altria Group, Inc., by Jim Gregory, April 3, 2002.

Jonathan Martin, Pamela L. Shelton, "Philip Morris Companies,
    Inc.," *International Directory of Company Histories*, 1997.

"Philip Morris USA Will Ask U.S. Supreme Court to Review Oregon
    Smoking Case Verdict," Altria, Media, Press Release, Dec. 26,
    2002.

Press release, "Philip Morris Companies, Inc., Announces Proposal to
    Change Name of Parent Company," Nov. 15, 2001.

Surgeon General's Reports, www.cdc.gov/tobacco/01sgrlst_temp.htm.

"The History of Philip Morris," About Philip Morris, www.philip
    morris.com.

Geoffrey C. Bible, "New Corporate Name," Philip Morris Companies
    Inc. Inter-Office Correspondence, Nov. 15, 2001, http://pmcos.
    pmmc.com/Link_Template.asp?name=011115_Bible_Desktop.
    htm.

Gene Borio, Tobacco Timeline, www.tobacco.org/History/Tobacco_
    History.htmlnday.

Michael Buettner, "Philip Morris Becomes Altria," Associated Press,
    The Detroit News, April 26, 2002, http://detnews.com/2002/
    business/0204/26/b03-475007.htm.

John A. Byrne, "Philip Morris," *BusinessWeek*, Nov. 29, 1999.

Seth Lubove, "Brand Power," *Forbes*, Aug. 9, 1999.

Anthony J. Sebok, "Why the Tobacco Class-Action Verdict Was Made,
    and What It Means," CNN.com, May 29, 2003.

Patricia Sellers, "Rising from the Smoke," *Fortune*, April 16, 2001.

Best Practice No. 6

Be Bold

I t takes a special kind of company to take a calculated risk with its corporate brand. Normally, we think of insurance companies as being risk-averse . . . but supplemental insurer AFLAC surprised everyone, including themselves, with a move so bold, it gave the company wings.

As a result of its new corporate identity, AFLAC enjoys virtually universal name recognition in the United States—not bad for a company that sells its products primarily to managers in small and mid-size businesses.

Increased familiarity, as we know, leads to increased favorability, and AFLAC has enjoyed not just rising recognition, but increased sales and stock price.

> *For AFLAC, the year 2000 was the year of the duck.*
> —Matthew Quinn,
> *Atlanta Journal and Constitution*

The unlikely vehicle for this success? A duck whose quack sounds unmistakably like "AFLAC!"

AFLAC
AN ODD DUCK, BUT AN EFFECTIVE ONE

Here's the cartoon. There's a guy standing in his kitchen, and he's peeking into the oven. From the oven, one word comes out: "AFLAC!" And the guy says, "I guess we're having duck for dinner."

Then there's this little item from *People* magazine: What is the difference between Ben Affleck and the AFLAC duck? For one thing, the AFLAC duck has never laid an egg . . . and Ben Affleck was in *Reindeer Games.*

So how did a company in the admittedly non-sexy industry of supplemental insurance wind up being compared favorably to the star of *The Sum of All Fears?*

As Groucho Marx might have said, it's the duck.

Before AFLAC introduced its spokesduck on December 31st, 1999, not too many people outside of the insurance industry were familiar with AFLAC, let alone the term *supplemental insurance.* But since then, the company's name recognition has skyrocketed—from 2 percent in 1990 to 80 percent in 2001. Sales increased as well, from $555 million in 1999 to $712 million in 2000, and to $919 million in 2001.

In February 2002, *Forbes* ranked AFLAC 112th in its Platinum list of America's Best Big Companies. In March 2002, *Fortune* included AFLAC in its list of most admired insurance companies.

The American Family Life Assurance Company (AFLAC, for short) was founded long before the duck, in 1955, by the three Amos brothers: John, Paul, and William. Originally created to sell general-purpose health, life, and accident insurance, the company suffered from a lack of distinction and seemed destined to fall fast into bankruptcy. But when the Amoses' father became stricken by cancer, the brothers were inspired to develop a unique new offering. In 1958,

AFLAC introduced the world's first cancer insurance policy: Within 1 year the company logged in almost $1 million worth of cancer insurance premiums.

Over time, AFLAC broadened the types of insurance it offers. It still sells policies that cover cancer treatments and related expenses, but the variety of product offerings, including accident, short-term disability, and dental insurance, has expanded, so that now AFLAC is one of the largest sellers of supplemental insurance in the United States.

In 1970, a visit to the World's Fair in Osaka provided CEO John Amos with some surprising insights into the Japanese insurance industry. He learned that the national healthcare plan left Japanese cancer patients financially exposed; in 1974 AFLAC became one of the first U.S. insurance companies to enter the Japanese market.

Today, Japan accounts for 76 percent of AFLAC Incorporated's pretax insurance earnings.

As Kathelen Spencer, AFLAC's Director of Corporate Communications, told us, "Our Japan story is really interesting. The government there makes it very difficult to enter the market, but once you do, they have certain protections to help you to succeed. Once they were satisfied that we were offering a legitimate product and had the financial resources to back up our sales, pay our claims, and so forth, we were given a period of exclusivity. During that time, we were able to expand our distribution system and consolidate our customer base, so that when other companies did enter the market we were the market leader."

Ironically, John Amos died of cancer himself in 1990. His nephew Dan became CEO; 2 years later he officially changed the name of the company to its acronym, largely because so many other companies in a variety of industries used the name "American." (The former name remains in use in Japan, largely because of the popularity of the American Family brand name.)

The name change also tacitly acknowledged that while the ultimate U.S. consumer might be the "American family," the real customers were other companies, businesses that offer their employees insurance plans as part of the corporate benefits package.

Kathelen Spencer explains, "For us, the first sale has to be made to the gatekeeper of the account. They're the ones who say, 'Yes, you may come in and offer this to our employees, and we will give you a payroll deduction spot.' Depending on the size of the company, that gatekeeper could be the business owner, it could be his wife who writes the payroll checks, it could be a payroll supervisor, or a benefits manager, or a vice president of HR, or a benefits consultant in a large account."

While AFLAC continued to dominate the Japanese supplemental insurance market, things in the United States were quite a bit sleepier. The company realized that it had to raise its domestic profile. In 1999, AFLAC began talking with Linda Kaplan Thaler, of the Kaplan Thaler Group in New York.

The agency created a campaign that, as Kathelen Spencer relates, "was very contrarian to the kinds of insurance advertising that people were seeing, which was about lifestyle protection and security, that kind of thing. Our campaign was disruptive in a way, because it introduced humor, it made fun of the fact that our name was somewhat difficult to remember, and it created a mnemonic device for reinforcing our name."

That campaign featured the AFLAC duck. Spencer says the duck "has the right answer, but nobody is listening, and that's a situation that resonates with people. There's also something inherently comical about a duck."

That's a point of difference in a world where insurance is marketed as a stable rock or a protective umbrella.

AFLAC regional sales coordinator Lisa Brennan told a reporter that "Everybody knows those duck commercials. People literally quack at us and say, 'You're the duck people.' "

According to Chairman and CEO Daniel P. Amos, at corporate headquarters recent history is viewed, not entirely tongue-in-cheek, as "B.D." and "A.D.": Before Duck and After Duck.

Figure 13-1. Storyboard: Yogi Berra meets the AFLAC duck. (Used with permission of AFLAC Incorporated. All rights reserved.)

In an interview with the *Atlanta Journal and Constitution*, Amos summed up the advertising's power like this: "If someone wants to sell you insurance, it's 'I'm sorry, I don't need any insurance.' And a wall goes up. But when we tell people we're AFLAC, they say, 'Oh, you're the company with the AFLAC duck,' and the wall comes down." We've included a storyboard for one of AFLAC's commercials in Figure 13-1—although chances are, you've already seen it on TV!

Amos attributes the company's sales growth to its expanding product line, plus an increasing distribution network of qualified reps and workplace customers. But as S&P Equity group analyst Cathy Seifert noted to *Investor's Business Daily*, "The ad campaign really raised AFLAC's profile." AFLAC backed the ads with a serious amount of cash. In 2000–2001 the company spent $80 million in advertising—up from $37 million in 1999.

The duck's distinctive squawk quickly became AFLAC's corporate ID. As Kathelen Spencer told us, "Insurance is regulated on a state-by-state basis, so even though our commercials describe what supplemental insurance does, they are not product specific and, therefore, remain in the category of institutional advertising. We choose national advertising vehicles, to keep it on the corporate or institutional level, so that we can run the same ad everywhere.

"We've really never done a product campaign," Spencer continues. "If you start naming kinds of products or getting very specific, since each state may have some variation on that, you get bogged down in having to run something that looks like the end of a car commercial, with all the legal lines. So we've sought to convey the general idea of why you need supplemental insurance, but without getting into the details of what any particular product does. And luckily, there are some general principles and concepts behind the whole philosophy of it that have made it applicable across the board."

The campaign also had a positive effect on AFLAC's CoreBrand Power. Between 1997 and 2001, the company's CoreBrand Power increased from 17 to 25 . . . almost a 50 percent increase. Looking

The Best of Branding

CoreBrand Power 1997 - 2001

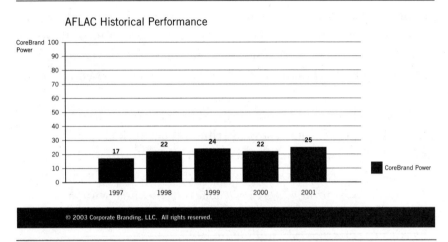

Figure 13-2. CoreBrand Power 1997–2001, AFLAC Historical Data

Familiarity and Favorability 1997 - 2001

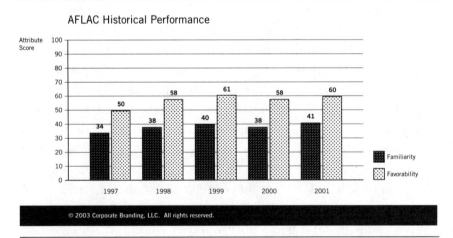

Figure 13-3. Familiarity and Favorability, 1997–2001, AFLAC Historical Data

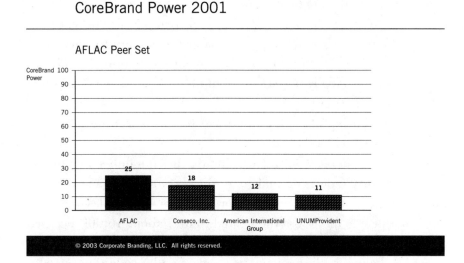

CoreBrand Power 2001

AFLAC Peer Set

Figure 13-4. CoreBrand Power 2001, AFLAC Peer Group

just at 2001, it's clear that AFLAC's familiarity, the result of that ubiquitous, loud AFLAC duck—was lifting its overall CoreBrand Power over the competition. You can see the comparisons in Figures 13-2, 13-3, and 13-4.

Interestingly, AFLAC's CoreBrand Power score dipped a bit in 2000, the year the duck came on board. The mixed reaction was illustrated by a *Wall Street Journal* review of "Madison Avenue's best and worst in 2000." While the reviewer called the AFLAC duck "arrogant" and "annoying," she went on to say that the campaign had boosted sales by 27 percent since its launch in January 2000. (In 2002, the *Journal* noted that the "obnoxious" duck was "still on a roll"—and once again, cited the campaign as an "advertising winner" for the year.)

AFLAC's 2001 Annual Report states that the advertising had an even greater impact on awareness: The AFLAC duck was known to an amazing 91 percent of potential customers.

The duck even boosted the company's stock price, although the company has had a long record of favorable earnings.

Kathelen Spencer says, "We've had real consistent earnings growth, between 15 and 17 percent, and a compound growth rate over the last 20 years of well over 20 percent on an annualized basis. It's been a good, steady investment. But in 2000, our stock was up 53 percent over the year before."

The advertising also plays a critical role in recruiting new sales agents . . . the lifeblood of AFLAC's sales.

Spencer explains, "Our advertising reaches not only our ultimate consumers, or the decision makers in the accounts, but is also a very important part of our recruiting effort in terms of our sales force. We have salespeople all across the United States, about 46,000 licensed agents, and in some places we are underpenetrated. So, as the advertising has helped with our name awareness and recognition, it's also elevated awareness among potential salespeople."

As a result, Spencer says, "That has really come on strongly in our recruiting numbers, as well as our sales numbers. So we can certainly attribute a significant role in the advertising to our increases."

In fact, the average monthly number of producing sales agents—those who write policies—increased 22 percent from 1999 to 2000. And those sales agents seemed to produce a disproportionate gain in revenue: In the first half of 2000 alone, new sales rose 24.5 percent.

The duck has even made it to Japan. (Even though there was a small translation problem: In Japan a duck says "ga-ga" instead of "quack.") While the U.S. ad campaign was designed to be a corporate umbrella, as Kathelen Spencer explains, "Our advertising in Japan has been product specific. I'm not sure if they feel like they can broaden the use of the duck to more of a corporate symbol, or if they think it has a better role for a particular product."

Of course, in Japan, AFLAC, or rather "American Family," is already the market leader, and has been for years. Spencer says, "We have got very high name recognition in Japan. In one newspaper survey, it was the highest among any foreign financial services company, higher than Merrill Lynch or Citibank. The name recognition is with 'American Family'—our original name until 1990—because there that's a very distinctive name. We've tried to move them toward using AFLAC, but the American Family name works so well because it is a point of distinction there."

Maintaining the duck as a brand symbol, both in the United States and Japan, takes vigilance.

Spencer says, "To preserve the longevity we have to spend a fair amount of time telling people, 'no, they can't put the duck in a costume, they can't have him saying anything else.' There are lots of rules and regulations about maintaining the duck's character. Certain images can go on a shirt, certain ones can't . . . I never imagined I'd spend my time being the policeman of the duck!"

Almost inadvertently, the duck—like Ronald McDonald before him—has become a symbol of support for pediatric cancer care.

In keeping with its original mission of cancer care—still an important part of AFLAC's core business—the company began a long-term sponsorship of a pediatric cancer center, called the AFLAC Cancer Center, at Children's Healthcare of Atlanta. The renovation and expansion afforded by AFLAC's initial $3 million contribution made the center the largest children's cancer center in the Southeast and one of the largest pediatric cancer centers in the United States. The young patients are treated for leukemia and other cancers, as well as blood diseases such as hemophilia and sickle cell disease.

"About 4 or 5 months into the duck campaign," Spencer recounts, "we started getting a lot of requests: Where can I buy the duck? Do you have anything with the duck on it? So we developed the idea of having a little duck shop. One of the items we have is a little 6-inch stuffed duck; when you squeeze it, it says 'AFLAC!'

"We said that we would donate the proceeds of anything sold over the Internet to the AFLAC Cancer Center," Spencer continues. "One day, Dan Amos was doing an interview on CNBC with Bill Griffith, and they kept quacking the duck. In the course of the interview, Dan had an opportunity to mention that sales over the Internet would go to the cancer center. We got so many orders that first day, it totally shut down the Web site, but we've overcome that. Developing a secondary identity for the duck as a link with our corporate philanthropy is something that I think is going to help with its longevity."

But duck or no duck, there is plenty of substance behind the style. In his "Message from Management" in the 2001 Annual Report, Dan Amos wrote, "Our objective for 2002 and 2003 is to increase operating earnings per share 15% to 17%. . . . Our optimism is based on AFLAC's strong position in the two largest insurance markets in the world."

Amos believes that the company's optimism is well-founded: "With our expertise at the worksite, our valuable but affordable products, and our outstanding customer service, we are confident that employees in both countries will continue to ask about AFLAC at work."

Notes

"AFLAC—Not Just a One-Product Company," ABI/Inform, Sept. 2000, Bell & Howell Information & Learning.

"Field Guide to Celebrities," *People*.

AFLAC Incorporated, Annual Report for 2001.

AFLAC Incorporated, Company Capsule, Hoover's Online, www.hoovers.com.

Interview with Kathelen Spencer, Director of Corporate Communications, AFLAC, by Jim Gregory, March 20, 2002.

Vance Cariaga, "Quackery? Insurer AFLAC Maintains Talking Duck Is Boosting Its Sales," *Investor's Business Daily*, Oct. 27, 2000.

Theresa Howard, "AFLAC Duck Gives Wings to Insurer's Name Recognition," *USA Today*, May 17, 2001.

Matthew Quinn, "Columbus, Ga.–Based Insurer Profits from Successful Advertising Campaign," *Atlanta Journal and Constitution*, May 20, 2001.

Suzanne Vranica, "Hard Sell: In 2000 Ad Year, Good Taste Was Optional," *Wall Street Journal.*

Suzanne Vranica and Vanessa O'Connel, "2002 Ads: Cheer Up!," *Wall Street Journal*, December 19, 2002.

Chapter Fourteen | Best Practice No. 7

Be Consistent

Generations of consumers grew up watching Ol' Lonely, the Maytag Repairman. Along with such brand icons as Tony the Tiger and the Jolly Green Giant, Ol' Lonely is one of the best-known personalities in advertising history. He represents his brand so well, that sometimes his personality has helped to overshadow some of the Maytag Corporation's real problems.

Maytag's investment in Ol' Lonely has spanned over 36 years. The payoff? The Maytag brand enjoys tremendous familiarity in terms of CoreBrand Power and the highest overall reputation of its peer group.

Although the Maytag Repairman made his debut during the Johnson administration, he hasn't stayed quite the same. As the brand and its message have evolved, he's been a teacher, a mediator between warring clans of parents and children, and of course, his ol', lonely self.

> *Our brands have earned the trust of families and business owners for more than a century. Nowhere is that better captured than in the Maytag Repairman.*
> —Former CEO Len Hadley,
> Annual Business Meeting Presentation, May 10, 2001

By 2001, Ol' Lonely had become a mentor to the next generation of Maytag men. Maytag Repairmen: We salute you.

MAYTAG
AN ENDURING—AND EVOLVING—
BRAND PERSONALITY

Viewers who tuned in to the *Today* show to watch Barbara Walters and Hugh Downs one morning in 1967 also got to see something new and different: the debut of one of the most enduring brand icons in American history. That icon was the Lonely Repairman, the Maytag Man. Thirty-six years later, the Lonely Repairman is still on the air, but he isn't working alone anymore. He has an eager young apprentice . . . and thereby hangs a tale.

Maytag has its roots in the nineteenth century, when Frederick L. (F. L.) Maytag and three colleagues created the Parson's Bandcutter and Self Feeder Company in Newton, Iowa. The company manufactured feeder attachments for grain threshing machines. By 1902 they had become the world's largest manufacturers of threshing machine feeders.

In 1909 F. L. Maytag took sole control of the operation, now named Maytag, and began tinkering with the idea of improving the old-fashioned wooden tub washer. Two years earlier, Maytag had introduced the company's first washing machine, a mechanical washer with a hand-crank mechanism. In 1911, Maytag introduced its first electric clothes washer, and 3 years later, a gas-powered model for homes without electricity. The new washing machines created so much consumer demand that Maytag eventually gave up on the thresher business and began making washers full time.

For most of its history, Maytag stood for one thing: reliability. In 1961, an ad created by Maytag's longtime advertising agency, Leo Burnett, appeared in *Life* magazine. Readers saw a picture of a woman who declared, "Got married in 1934. Got Maytag in 1936. Both Marriage and Maytag still working."

The introduction of "Ol' Lonely" on the *Today* show was in a commercial called "The Drill Instructor." The spot, also from Leo Burnett, featured the Lonely Repairman training a group of young assistants how to inspect each machine . . . and how to fill up their time with knitting and crosswords, since all the Maytags they were responsible for were working just fine.

But in more recent times, however, dependability wasn't just the provenance of Maytag anymore. Consumers had come to expect their appliances to work reliably, no matter who made them. In a 2000 test, a *Consumer Reports* panel rated 11 washing machines from different manufacturers: six of the models were judged to be "excellent," and the other five were "very good."

Despite the parity of perception on dependability, Maytag was asking consumers to pay a premium for its brand. In 1996, when 40 percent of washers sold for less than $399, the lowest-priced Maytag machine cost $439.

As a result, in the mid-1990s, Maytag found that its brand awareness and its consideration by consumers had reached a ceiling. In the words of Bill Beer, President of Maytag Appliances (a division that includes the Maytag brand, as well as Jenn-Air, Amana, and Magic Chef brands), "Our brand awareness level was kind of maxing out."

Maytag has tracked its brand since 1974. As Bill Beer describes it, the company evaluates its brand consideration, or brand equity, on four different levels.

- **Awareness:** Do consumers know the brand name?
- **Consideration:** Consumers know Maytag makes washing machines. Would they consider our brand with the rest of their options?
- **Brand preference:** If you could choose any brand of clothes washer you wanted, which brand would you choose?
- **Conviction:** This is the one, Beer says, "that we're really attempting to achieve. It says, 'I'm not going out to buy a new washing machine. I'm going out to buy a new Maytag.' It's the conviction that the consumer won't accept any substitute."

"We started feeling like the advertising and the image and every-thing else was a bit dated, a bit stodgy, a bit conservative," Beer says, "and we weren't translating brand awareness, which was high, into brand preference."

Even so, the Maytag brand name was strong. Surveys showed that 45 percent of consumers preferred the Maytag brand of washers and dryers. Yet Maytag's actual share of market was only 15 percent.

Clearly, consumers loved the Maytag name, but not its premium price. If dependability could be found in any washer, why pay more for a Maytag?

Maytag had gotten its potential consumers up to the second level of its four-level scale. The next job was to move consumers into brand preference, and from that, conviction.

Then-CEO Lloyd Ward decided that the way to influence con-sumers to buy more Maytags was to add new benefits to the venerable brand, benefits that, as he said to the *Wall Street Journal*, consumers would be "willing to pay for."

So Maytag embarked on a series of product innovations, harking back to its earliest days of inventing the automatic clothes washer. In 1997, the company introduced the hugely popular Neptune line of front-loading washing machines. Underscoring its strides in design and product innovation, Maytag even partnered with fashion designer Nicole Miller to introduce some of its latest appliance models.

In addition to its product development, the company made a con-scious change in its advertising.

As Bill Beer told us, "We looked at our campaign, which I think is part of the secret of why we are where we are. We've had a very con-sistent, very constant campaign, running since 1967: that old Lonely Repairman campaign. And it's based on a very important product attribute, which is reliability or dependability.

"But," Beer continues, "we made a conscious decision in the mid-1990s to take our national advertising to a different level.

"If you look at our commercials prior to 1996 or 1997, the Repair-man was the hero of the commercial. In the mid-1990s, through 2001, our advertising still used the Lonely Repairman, but more in a cameo

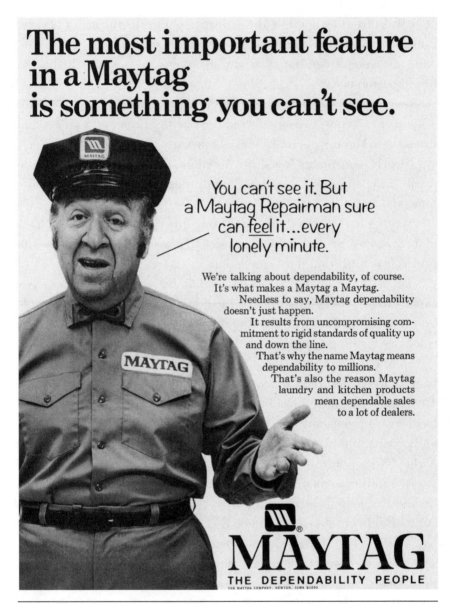

Figure 14-1. The Lonely Repairman has been Maytag's spokesman for over 35 years. (Source: Maytag Corporation.)

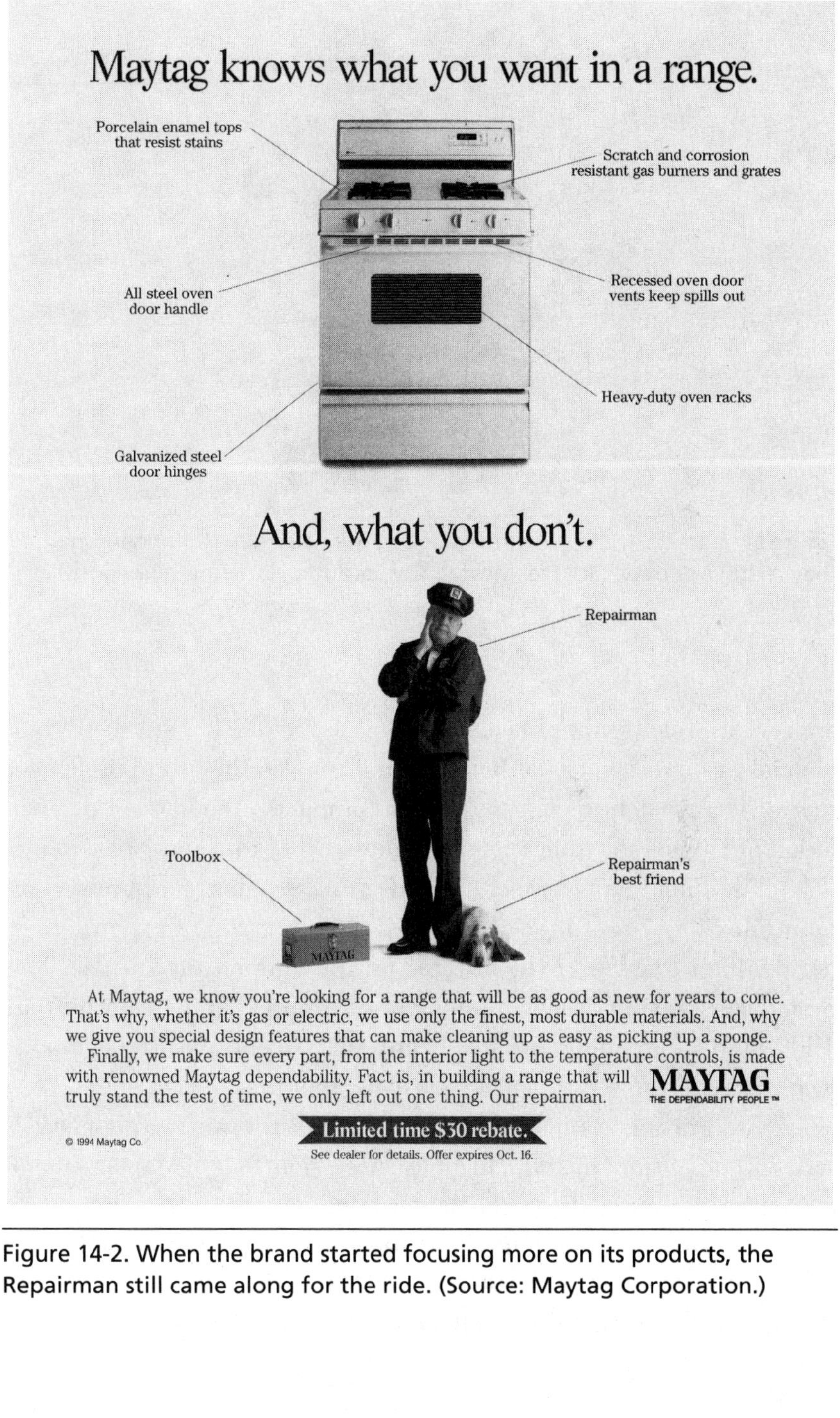

Figure 14-2. When the brand started focusing more on its products, the Repairman still came along for the ride. (Source: Maytag Corporation.)

Figure 14-3. In 2001, the Repairman got a junior partner. No longer lonely, they're still not busy. (Source: Maytag Corporation 2001 Annual Report.)

appearance role. And product started becoming the hero in these commercials, as opposed to the Repairman. It moved the brand preference scores: That switch in creative had that impact." You can see the evolution of Maytag's commercials in Figures 14-1, 14-2, and 14-3.

While the Maytag brand focused on its product, its parent company, Maytag Corporation, was engaged in a period of expansion—a period that turned out to be ill-fated for the company as a whole. This period cost Maytag dearly. Its stock price dropped 40 percent from its 1999 high, shareholder equity shrank 96 percent, and the company went through three different CEOs in 10 months.

To add insult to injury, Maytag's retail distribution experienced a series of convulsions in 2000. In quick succession, four of Maytag's major customers withdrew from the home appliance market. Circuit City announced it was going out of the home appliance business, Heiling-Meyers closed a third of its 900 stores, and both Montgomery Ward and Bradlee's went out of business altogether.

The biggest bright spot in the corporation's fortunes at this point was the acquisition of refrigerator giant Amana in 2001. Even so, while the purchase made Maytag an even greater force in the U.S. major appliance industry, the $300 million loan it needed to finance the purchase increased both long-term debt and interest payments.

Speaking at the company's 2001 Annual Meeting, then-CEO Len Hadley remarked: "If you were to read the mainstream business media, you might conclude that we are living in an era best described by the phrase of Charles Dickens, 'It was the best of times, it was the worst of times.' "

And yet despite the turmoil, Maytag remained an incredibly powerful brand. In terms of its CoreBrand Power scores, it barely registered a downward blip, despite its financial woes and management turnover. By 2001, Maytag's CoreBrand Power rating was the strongest it had ever been. Maytag's CoreBrand Power scores are shown in Figures 14-4, 14-5, and 14-6.

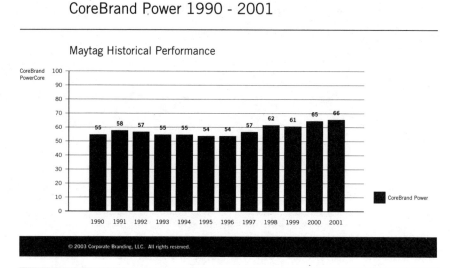

Figure 14-4. CoreBrandPower 1990–2001, Maytag Historical Performance.

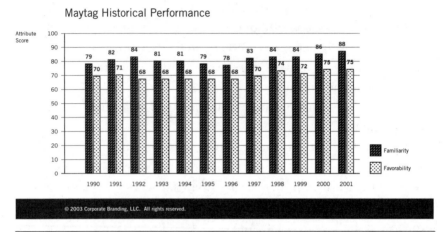

Figure 14-5. Familiarity and Favorability 1990–2001, Maytag Historical
Performance

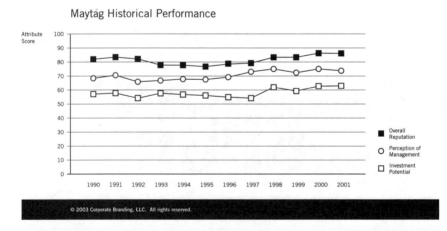

Figure 14-6. Favorability Attributes 1990–2001, Maytag Historical
Performance.

According to Bill Beer, this was because "our corporate brand is so overshadowed by the consumer brand view of the company.

"The umbrella brand positioning for Maytag has been built specifically on dependability, reliability, and durability," Beer says. "The personification of those attributes is the old Lonely Repairman. When consumers give us feedback about the brand, they don't talk about 'reliability and dependability,' but about trust, and a trusted brand.

"I believe that the corporate brand is probably in a stronger place today, because of that consumer perception of trust in the brand," Beer continues. "It's that personality and personification that add to the strength of this brand. I would give prior management and our advertising agency, Leo Burnett, our partners for 47 years now, a great deal of credit for the constancy of that message.

"I believe what's driving our brand strength is the fact that when you say Maytag, you see in your mind's eye, not necessarily a washing machine, but a repairman that doesn't have anything to do."

In 2001, Maytag introduced a new generation of advertising . . . and a new generation of repairmen.

Ol' Lonely gained an assistant, one more interested in product benefits and innovations than his mentor had ever been. The focus is back on brand, without neglecting the attributes that make consumers want to move from brand preference to brand conviction.

Bill Beer says, "Now, I happen to believe, when you're using the Repairman as a cameo instead of as a hero, you're borrowing from the equity of that long-standing commercial, not adding to it. So, if you looked at the first 30 years of that commercial as building equity in the Repairman, I would say we were extracting equity over the last 5 years and applying it to product. And now, we need to go back and put a little money back in the savings account, if you will, and bring the Repairman back into more of a role as the hero.

"So, in 2001, you saw us bring an apprentice to go along with the old Lonely Repairman. The story line came back more. We've still got product. But the advertising is again more about the Repairman without completely neglecting the product. We're trying to keep the best of both."

Notes

"Maytag Corporation," Hoover's Online, www.hoovers.com.

"Maytag Repairman Enters 21st Century—Old Lonely Gets Hunky Apprentice Who Wants to Work," *The Toronto Star*, Jan. 28, 2001.

"Ol' Lonely, The Maytag Man, Key Facts," News Bureau, Our Company, The Maytag Home, www.maytag.com.

Interview with Bill Beer, President, Maytag Appliances, and Chris Wegnall, Vice President of Marketing for Major Appliances, Maytag Appliances, by Jim Gregory, March 1, 2002.

The Today Show Scrapbook, http://www.msnbc.com/onair/nbc/today/scrapbook.

Lisa Bonnema, "Appliance Industry Forecasts: 2002: A Short, Bumpy Ride," Appliance Magazine.com.

Len Hadley, "Annual Meeting Business Presentation," Maytag, May 10, 2001.

Joseph T. Hallinan, "Can Laundry-King Maytag Make Balance Sheet Sparkle?" *Wall Street Journal*, March 15, 2000.

Carl Quintanilla, "Lloyd Ward Puts a New Spin on Maytag," *Wall Street Journal*, as it appeared in *The News-Times*, Nov. 26, 1996.

Chapter Fifteen | Best Practice No. 8

Communicate Your Corporate Brand 360 Degrees

Happy employees are good for business—they are more loyal and productive and thus, help make their companies more successful. The Principal Financial Group understands that premise better than anyone else: They provide the financial solutions that help people feel secure about their financial future. This simple thought is the heart of the company's brand strategy and business success and is expressed in all of the company's communications.

That corporate brand strategy is relatively new, replacing a campaign designed to convey a name change. Once the new name had a certain level of awareness, The Principal decided it was time to evolve their brand to the next level, developing the new brand to communicate the true strengths of their business.

One of the truly brilliant aspects of how The Principal has implemented its brand strategy is the way it is so clearly evident in every element of the company's behavior. This 360-degree approach to its corporate brand is reflected in everything from its corporate advertising to the many awards it receives for being a great place to work. The results show in record sales and earnings growth.

This synergy didn't happen by itself. It was created through strong interaction between senior management and a company-wide "communicators' network." It's also the result of paying attention to customers and regulators, and keeping close tabs on the competition.

Most of all, it comes from recognizing, protecting, and nurturing that valuable asset—the corporate brand.

> *How do you build a brand? The first thing you do is to earn your reputation.*
>
> —Mary O'Keefe, Senior Vice President,
> Corporate Relations and Human Resources,
> The Principal Financial Group

THE PRINCIPAL FINANCIAL GROUP
THEY UNDERSTAND WHAT YOU'RE WORKING FOR

In February 2002, for the seventh year in a row, *Fortune* magazine named The Principal Financial Group one of America's "most admired companies" within the Life and Health Insurance industry. The fact that this acknowledgment came only a year after The Principal went public "is a tribute to the quality and dedication of our employees," said Chairman, CEO, and President J. Barry Griswell. "Our focus on the customer, our integrity, and our people will continue to create success as a leader in financial products and services."

That's not the only honor The Principal has received. In October 2001, it was recognized by *Working Mother* magazine as one of the "100 Best Companies for Working Mothers," in recognition of its extensive work-life programs, flexible work schedules, and generous maternity benefits. In the same year, it received its fourth annual mention in *LatinaStyle* magazine as one of the top 50 companies offering professional opportunities for Hispanic women.

All this, plus record earnings growth. In 2000, operating earnings shot up an amazing 32 percent. The company has assets of nearly $118 billion and serves more than 13 million customers around the world. The Principal Financial Group is clearly doing a lot of things right.

Based in Des Moines, Iowa, The Principal Financial Group is the ninth-largest U.S. life insurance company, according to *Fortune* magazine. It's a leading provider of retirement savings, investment, and insurance products. In fact, according to *CFO* magazine, more employers choose The Principal for their 401(k) plans than any other bank, mutual fund, or insurance company in the United States.

The company's growth—and its reputation for being a great employer—stem from the heart of its brand strategy. In business for over 120 years, the company focuses on two key questions for its customers and employees alike:

- What are you working for?
- How can we help you get there?

The Principal was founded to provide reliable insurance coverage in less than reliable times. Shortly after the Civil War, several life insurance companies found that it was easier to be profitable if they cancelled policies before customers could be paid benefits. Edward Temple, a Civil War veteran and banker, founded Bankers Life in 1879 to provide dependable, affordable—and accessible—life insurance to his fellow bankers and their families.

The company grew steadily, despite the high death tolls of the global influenza epidemic of 1918–1919 and the two World Wars. The company's financial resources were inevitably strained as it paid policyholder claims for lives lost in those tragedies.

After World War II, however, the company began a sharper growth curve, adding new product lines to its life insurance business, including retirement funding products (1946), group health insurance (1952), and mutual funds (1968).

In 1985, in recognition of its expanded product lines, and to facilitate future growth, Bankers Life changed its name to The Principal Financial Group. Today, The Principal is made up of four primary business units: (1) Retirement and Investment Services, which provides retirement savings plans to businesses for their employees worldwide; (2) Life and Health Insurance, which offers individual life insurance and group life and health plans; (3) Institutional Asset

Management, which provides investment services to large corporate, employee group, and foundation retirement funds; and (4) Mortgage Banking, which provides and services residential mortgage loans.

The new name required a new look and logo. As Mary O'Keefe, Senior Vice President, Corporate Relations and Human Resources, told us, "We selected a blue triangular shape for the new logo. We called it 'the edge,' because of its shape and because it refers to the advantage we bring to our customers. We saw the theme as giving customers 'an edge' on a secure financial future."

But in an insurance market full of recognizable symbols—MetLife's Snoopy, for one—the "edge" was a challenging icon to bring to life.

O'Keefe remembers the challenge of branding the new identity: "We took the edge of the triangular logo and brought it into the theme, 'Get an Edge with The Principal,' our original tagline. Our advertising agency at the time came up with the idea of morphing common, everyday items—a Swiss army knife, lifesavers, coins, a calculator, and so on—into the triangle shape of the logo to represent particular product lines. This focused attention on the new logo and built awareness for the company. The ads helped shape the message that The Principal was a force in its key businesses: life insurance, employee benefits, mortgages, and, most importantly, retirement services."

As O'Keefe recalls, "We felt that if we could present the logo to people in a unique way, it would be more memorable. The idea of the advertising was to continually reinforce the name and logo of the company. We were not as large a company, and at that time, we weren't a public company. We really had to work at getting that identity out there. I think our success shows the importance of choosing a strong branding idea and sticking with it. By concentrating on the shape of the logo, it became a recognizable symbol for our company and brought us a presence in the marketplace." See Figure 15-1 for a sample of The Principal's "The Edge" campaign.

Over time, The Principal felt it needed to focus its efforts on a market in which it had always had a unique advantage: providing services

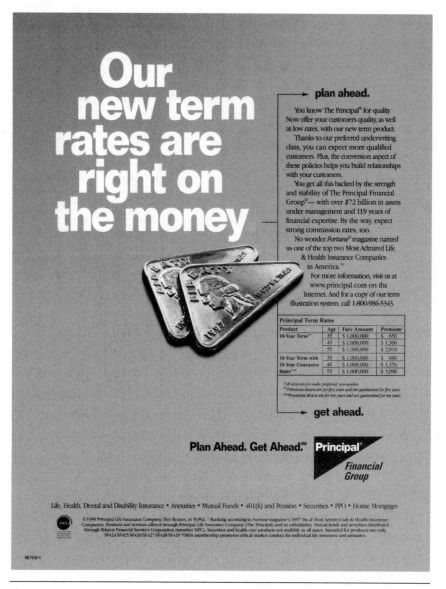

Figure 15-1. The Principal's "The Edge" campaign transformed everyday objects into a reminder of the Principal triangle. (©2003 Principal Financial Services, Inc. Used with permission.)

to small and medium-size companies. While The Principal also provides services to individuals and large companies, its relationships with small and medium-size businesses are, as Mary O'Keefe puts it, "our bread and butter."

About a dozen years after the introduction of "The Principal Edge," market research showed that it was time for a change. O'Keefe says, "We found that our name was recognized by a great majority of small and medium business owners, but when we dug more deeply and asked, 'What do you know about The Principal beyond the logo, triangular-shaped objects, and the name?' people didn't know what we do and what we stand for. They had a generally favorable opinion of us, but couldn't explain why they felt that way.

"We felt that we had done our job in making the name and logo recognized, but it was time to better define what the company stands for," O'Keefe continues. "So if a client company says, 'I love the 401(k) plan from The Principal, and I wish I could find a life and health insurer that's just as good,' we need to make sure they know that they can still rely on The Principal. We want them to know the depth of our services.

"Our communications still contribute to the awareness and recognition of the company," O'Keefe says, "but now we're also influencing the knowledge people have and the way they feel about us, so that our targets will say: 'I'm familiar with The Principal. I know what they do. And I feel good about the company.'"

The theme of the new branding campaign for The Principal is "We understand what you're working for." As O'Keefe describes it, "Whether you're a business trying to be successful or an individual planning for your future, we'll get in and work with you to help you achieve your goals."

Where the previous advertising focused on developing awareness of the company, the new campaign squarely targets the emotional and psychological aspects of doing business with The Principal.

The campaign is designed to speak to owners and senior managers of small and medium-size businesses, who make decisions about retirement plans, life and health insurance programs, and other benefits to offer their employees. The idea is that these benefits will help the companies attract and retain good employees as they improve employees' quality of life. As one ad boldly promises, "Take this job and love it." Figure 15-2 shows another ad from this campaign.

David Wozniak, Director of Advertising for The Principal, has fielded research on the campaign since it was introduced in August of 2000. "Our various target audiences have let us know that the advertising is memorable, breakthrough, and unique to the industry," Wozniak told us. "And it's really beginning to enhance the personality of the organization. People are understanding what business we're in, and where we have our stake in the ground."

Mary O'Keefe adds, "How do you build a brand? From our standpoint, the first thing you do is to earn your reputation. You do the right things to earn a good reputation. And then you tell people what it stands for and you build your brand on that reputation. Lots of elements go into building a strong brand. Consistency is important, so one of the things that we've developed is a 'one-look' program. The idea is that although we're an organization engaged in a number of diverse businesses, we want people to be able to pick up any of the communications we've developed and know it's from The Principal."

To make sure that people throughout the company have a stake in the brand and marketing materials, The Principal brought together roughly 100 communications professionals from throughout the organization and formed "the communicators' network." The people in the network are responsible for holding up the brand's image and presenting key messages in every internal and external piece of communication. The Principal has instituted a number of strategies to keep the people in the network informed and empowered to do their jobs.

Mary O'Keefe says, "While creating our advertising and public relations is centralized in our Corporate Relations department, all of our business units have communications people who are responsible for creating collateral marketing materials for their specific product lines. Our communicators' network meets once a month, so we can keep our branding themes and key messages at the forefront of people's minds. And we ask those communicators to participate with us

Figure 15-2. The Principal's new campaign emphasized the company's key benefit: happy employees. (©2003 Principal Financial Services, Inc. Used with permission.)

in developing the 'one-look' so that they'll have ownership and use it in their own materials. We will be having a communicators' conference in the near future to create even more of a sense of partnership."

The Principal has an extensive style guide, or as David Wozniak calls it, "a brand document," which is a continually updated reference tool for the writers and artists in the communicators' network. As Wozniak explains, "There's a constant need for ongoing education as to why consistency is important to building the brand. And we have to help people understand how everything that they're doing relates back to the overall brand."

Communication also plays a key role in employee satisfaction. "Interestingly," Mary O'Keefe comments, "we work just as hard at our internal communications—building our 'employment brand'—as we do with communications to our customers. Our theme, 'we understand what you're working for,' is perfect for our internal audiences as well as our customers. We do a lot of education with our employees. We tell the folks on the front line what we're doing and remind them that reinforcing and building the brand is their responsibility too."

In addition, senior management helps determine the direction of the brand. Their input is vital to interpreting the brand theme, communicating the direction of the company, and representing business objectives.

Mary O'Keefe explains, "We meet on a regular basis with our senior management group, the people who run the different business units. It's not just the CEO. It's not just the communications people. We sit with our business leaders and find out the needs of their businesses. Then we're able to come to an agreement about interpreting the branding theme for their benefit, developing our key messages, determining how we're going to weigh our messages in terms of spending, how we're going to pay for it, and what our measures of success will be."

The Principal had expanded its product offerings in 1998, when it introduced Principal Bank, a virtual chartered bank that allows customers to do their banking via the Internet, on the phone, or through the mail. In 1999, Principal Bank added a credit card, which the *Northwestern Financial Review* dubbed "a major success." One of the fastest-growing banking organizations in the country, Principal Bank was profitable after only 20 months. After its first 4 years in business, it already had over $1 billion in assets. Principal Bank President and CEO Barrie Christman attributed the bank's success to "being associated with a strong brand and customer loyalty of The Principal Financial Group."

Like many others in its industry, The Principal took another key business step in 2001 when it became a publicly traded company, positioning itself for even more growth.

At The Principal, supporting the brand is manifested in all areas of the business. For instance, The Principal offers a full line of insurance and investment products, through community banks, for the banks' small-business clients. This provides another opportunity to reinforce its brand strategy—helping small to medium-size companies realize their goals. Even its charitable contributions fall in line with the brand: After the disasters of September 11, The Principal contributed $250,000 to the World Trade Center Small Business Recovery Fund.

Only time will tell how becoming a public company—and expanding its portfolio of services—will affect The Principal as a business. But what won't change is the company's commitment to its brand. As Mary O'Keefe says, "We try to be very consistent in our core messages and our core values. The brand reflects these messages and values. I don't see any change in those."

Notes

"Banks and Insurers Cross Over in US," *Life Insurance International*, Aug. 31, 2000.

"Capitalizing on Brand Name, Principal Bank Turns First Profit," *Northwestern Financial Review*, Feb. 5, 2000.

"News Room—Corporate," www.principal.com.

"The Principal Financial Group Named One of America's Most Admired Companies," *Business Wire*, Feb. 26, 2002.

"What Are You Working For?" 2000 Annual Report, The Principal Financial Group.

Company Profile: The Principal Financial Group," Hoover's Online, www.hoovers.com.

Interview with Ed Brown, Brown Marketing Communications, by Jim Gregory, Feb. 28, 2002.

Interview with Mary O'Keefe and David Wozniak, The Principal Financial Group, by Jim Gregory, Feb. 28, 2002.

Principal Bank, About Us, http://www.principal.com/bank/aboutus. htm.

Vince Calio, "Principal to Market Online Retail Banking Services to Participants," *Defined Contribution News*, Jan. 1, 2001.

Fran Matso Lysiak, "Principal Financial Group Acquires Executive Benefit Services," *Best's Insurance News*, Jan. 23, 2001.

Ron Panko, "The Second Wave—Demutualization," *Best's Review*, April 1, 2001.

David Reich-Hale, "Starting Small, Principal Taps Banks," *American Banker*, June 4, 2001.

Best Practice No. 9

Own Your Industry's Innovations

IBM didn't get it. When the PC revolution started, bringing computing power to home and office desktops around the world, IBM was still thinking mainframes. While other companies began to get the edge in sexy new hardware and user-friendly software, IBM was focusing on small, niche product lines—and thinking about breaking up Big Blue altogether.

Enter Lou Gerstner. This veteran marketer decided not only to hold IBM together but to take the lead in the industry's next big development: e-business.

> *We've stayed true to our focus, which is that e-business and the Internet are about real business . . . it's about transforming your enterprise.*
>
> —Lou Gerstner, former Chairman and CEO, IBM

IBM
REINVENTING A BRAND—AND REVITALIZING A BUSINESS

In a decade of unprecedented technological change, IBM reinvented itself not only to be part of the revolution, but to lead it.

In 1990, IBM was riding high. Maureen McGuire, IBM's Vice President of Worldwide Marketing Management and Integrated Marketing Communications, describes IBM in the 1980s and early 1990s as "a large, almost unstoppable, successful company. You know, you'll never get fired for buying IBM."

According to our own data, no other company among the thousand we survey each year has ever reached IBM's 1990 levels of Core-Brand Power, driven by a combination of reputation, perception of management, and investment potential.

IBM had been a business superpower for almost 80 years, building ever bigger and ever smarter machines. Its clients were large organizations with big "glass house" information technology (IT) operations and a limited number of top executives who could sign checks for high-end purchases: the head of the IT operation, the CFO, and the CEO.

As McGuire says, "These were customers who knew IBM very well. Nobody else had a relationship with IBM, and nobody else needed to."

But something had begun to happen on the periphery of IBM's collective vision. The PC revolution had started, shifting the market to distributed computing and client servers. And, most significantly, the buyers changed. No longer limited to C-level executives, IT buying decisions were suddenly being made by many people in many different places inside organizations.

"With the onset of the PC, people were buying their own desktops," says McGuire, "and I don't think our management system was ready for it."

The whole era of distributed computing, a sea change in the industry, caught IBM unawares.

The company hit a new low at the end of 1992. On December 31st of that year, IBM released a shocking two-page ad in the *Wall Street Journal*, followed by publication in the *New York Times* and 10 other journals. The headline read: "What's Really Going On at IBM?" The ad was an attempt to explain IBM's announcement, 2 weeks earlier, that it would report the biggest loss in its 78-year history, eliminate 25,000 jobs, and trim $1 billion from development and overhead. By

December 17th, IBM's shareholders lost a collective $6 billion as their stock plunged $11 per share.

By early 1993, IBM's reputation had slipped significantly; the market's perception of the company's management and investment potential plunged to half of what it had been a mere 2 years before. Clearly, IBM was still a big player in U.S. business, but the market increasingly saw it as a poor investment . . . and didn't trust management to pull out of the tailspin. In 1993, IBM, the fabled Big Blue, was on the brink of the unthinkable. It was close to going bankrupt.

That same year, Louis V. Gerstner, Jr. joined IBM as Chairman and CEO. Years later, speaking to Lou Dobbs on CNN, Gerstner recalled, "What I found in IBM was a company frozen. I mean it was like a huge, huge supertanker frozen in the ice in the Arctic."

Gerstner's dramatic first step was to cancel predecessor John Akers's scheme to break up IBM into a loose network of "Baby Blues" built around different products. Since the 1950s, IBM had been fragmenting itself into increasingly autonomous business groups. These divisions had the freedom to create their own identities, their own brands, even their own names, logos, and graphic standards. As a result, many IBM divisions were no longer recognizable to the public: Adstar offered data storage, Eduquest offered education products, and ISSC handled global services. The IBM name was being diluted . . . and the small niche brands were not going to get traction in an expanding marketplace.

Gerstner made a decision to change the nature of IBM at its very core. From that moment, IBM was going to be an integrator, a provider of business solutions. Instead of having multiple niche businesses within the IBM framework, IBM was going to be a "non-niche" player, with services, rather than products, driving the company forward.

By keeping the company together, Gerstner believed that he could offer corporate customers not only the trusted IBM name, but the widest range of products and experts in the business, a combination capable of addressing virtually any IT dilemma. But IBM would have a long way to go before Gerstner's vision would turn the company around.

IBM's research from this period showed that its target market saw them as arrogant, bureaucratic, and irrelevant. Maureen McGuire remembers that "Our customers still believed in the IBM brand, but they were mad at us for failing. They saw IBM as an icon of American success, and when we failed, that made them feel very nervous.

"But still and all, they saw us as a great company, with smart, trustworthy people. And we took notes."

In 1994, Gerstner took another crucial step in bringing his vision of IBM to life by hiring American Express veteran Abby F. Kohnstamm as Senior Vice President of Marketing. Kohnstamm immediately stepped up to the challenge Gerstner had created, dismissing IBM's 75 ad agencies and creating a powerful marketing partnership with global advertising leader Ogilvy & Mather. Between 1994 and 1999, IBM would invest $2 billion to change its image and integrate its brand message.

That first year, O&M introduced the "Solutions for a Small Planet" campaign, a series of vignettes showing how IBM technology could help people improve their lives. The people they portrayed were not the stuffy CIOs of yesteryear . . . they were young, old, local, global, the customers of the new distributed computing era. IBM even redesigned its Aptiva PCs, making them sleeker, sexier, more in line with the company's new image.

"When our ad campaign came out," McGuire says, "and showed we were paying attention, we began relatively quickly to see an uptick in our reputation. The campaign got people talking about IBM again, this time in a more positive way."

IBM was back in charge of what people were going to think of them, filling the vacuum created by years of doubt and increasing perceptions of irrelevance.

Hiring a single ad agency, and creating a single corporate voice, reenergized another critical IBM constituency: its employees.

According to McGuire, "The advertising did a lot to teach people internally at IBM that one voice was stronger than 25 voices. So while there was a lot of initial resistance to changing the trends of almost 50 years, there was recognition that something positive was happening . . . and bit by bit, people wanted to be part of that."

Gerstner sent other strong signals that IBM was back in charge of its own destiny. Internally, he ended a long period of "water torture" layoffs that had cut 150,000 jobs. The company made one more major cut of 35,000 employees, but made it clear that this would be the last for the foreseeable future. Employees' morale began to go up as their jobs became more secure and they saw the company taking steps to change its trajectory. Gerstner took a similar step for investors, taking a single big charge in late 1993.

Consolidating IBM's brand, voice, and management direction proved to have a strong economic value. By the end of 1993, IBM's favorability index had begun to creep upward, the first such sign in almost 2 years. The market's perception of management and IBM's investment potential was slowly beginning to change for the better. In 1994, IBM reported its first profit in 4 years.

In 1995, Gerstner introduced a new vision for the IT industry at the annual Comdex show in Las Vegas: He declared that the Internet would be about "business, not browsing." While many businesses saw the Internet as no more than a place to put a home page, Gerstner vowed that it would change the way business is done all over the world, integrating business processes, improving productivity, smoothing supply chains, and harmonizing interactions both internally and externally. The networked company would drive the next phase of industry growth. IBM called this new phenomenon "e-business."

Abby Kohnstamm defined e-business as "an operating principle that guides all the company's business practices, products, and services." Kohnstamm championed e-business as an organic concept—a living, breathing way of doing business, extending to customer relationships, service, procurement, and supply chain management.

IBM knew that to be the industry leader, it would have to set the standard.

Maureen McGuire told us how IBM embraced its own vision. "Every business unit had to consider how their products were going to play in the e-business revolution. And people began to get it, because it affected the hardware, the software, the services, the technology group—all the pieces of IBM were affected by this vision and this strategy.

"So it wasn't just a communications effort," McGuire continues. "It was real, in the plumbing of IBM, changing the way we do business and changing the way we develop our products and services so that our customers can do business better. We changed the way we did business by becoming an e-business ourselves."

Steve Gardner, co-founder of the Gardner-Nelson Project and—as President of ad agency Ammirati Martin Puris—one-time manager of the Compaq account, told *USA Today* that, "The most stunning thing about e-business was that it transformed IBM from perceived laggard to leader . . . without any real shift in its products and services."

Again, the vision had a tangible effect in the marketplace. By 1996, IBM's favorability attributes, while not completely recovered, were at the closest point to their all-time high in 1990, and the branding effort had added $50 million to IBM's increasing market value. You can see IBM's CoreBrand Power history from 1990–2001 in Figures 16-1, 16-2, and 16-3.

O&M introduced e-business to the public in a 1997 TV campaign. The ads told stories most customers could relate to: an international conference call flames out due to bad connections, a Web designer builds a hot logo but can't connect the home page to the rest of the Web site.

In each case, IBM offered its solution to the "e-problem," topping off each tale with its new signature, a witty red "e" logo. The TV spots

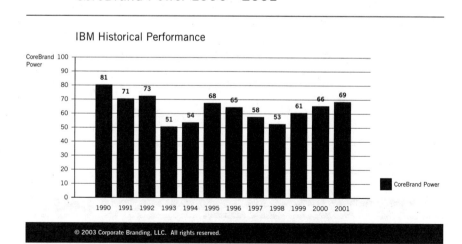

Figure 16-1. CoreBrand Power 1990–2001, IBM Historical Performance

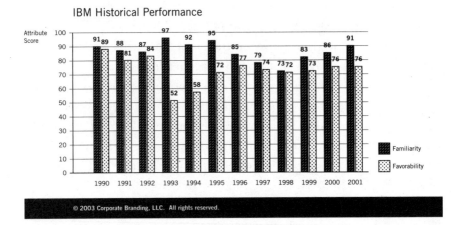

Figure 16-2. Familiarity and Favorability 1990–2001, IBM Historical Performance

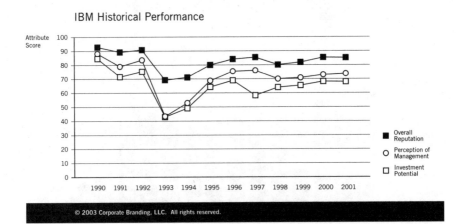

Figure 16-3. Favorability Attributes 1990–2001, IBM Historical Performance

Figure 16-4. IBM's ad campaign showed how it could help any company become an e-business. (Source: IBM Corporation)

were followed by a targeted print campaign, showing how IBM had helped companies from Macy's to Mercedes become e-businesses. Figure 16-4 shows an example of that print campaign.

IBM's ad campaign was just the tip of the iceberg. IBM and Ogilvy extended the e-business campaign into every facet of their communications, from advertising to events, direct marketing, Internet marketing, product design, and employee training.

Maureen McGuire says, "We really believe in integration and a 360-degree approach. We can't outspend our competition, so we have to make all of our dollars work together to get the message out. And it's not just about putting our name out there. It's about forming business relationships, in the United States and worldwide."

Shelly Lazarus, Chairman and CEO of O&M Worldwide, has been quoted as saying, "Five years ago, people would say that IBM has an incredible brain, but not a heart. Today, it has a brain and a soul and a sense of humor. It's as if they took off their jackets in the room."

Customers agreed.

"Look at what IBM stood for [in 1993]," said Peter Sealey, former marketing head at Coca-Cola. "It was stuffy, white shirts, big iron. Now the company is accessible. It's a wonderful example of an institution recasting itself."

IBM's next step was to further emphasize its service capabilities. In 1999, the company spent $75 million on advertising that showcased its consulting expertise (IBM Global Services). The ads featured short business bios and dramatic closeups of IBM employees, individually and in teams. The faces were quirky, friendly, smart, savvy; clearly, these were people customers could not only rely on, but relate to.

The tagline said it all: *IBM Global Services. People who think. People who do. People who get it.* Significantly, business hardware was nowhere in the advertising: It was understood that IBM's technology was unparalleled. The key was using the hardware and software to solve business problems . . . and IBM experts were the ones to do it.

Once again, IBM invested to put muscle behind its message, hiring thousands of consultants to join the Global Services division.

These consultants, with specific industry backgrounds, allowed IBM to offer increasingly higher levels of value to customers in such key areas as financial services and insurance. At the same time, IBM continued to improve and integrate its technology. And once again, the results showed. IBM's favorability attributes rose in unison, reflecting the increasing momentum of this IT powerhouse.

In 1993, Lou Gerstner had a vision that would transform IBM from a giant hardware store into the world's preeminent provider of business and technology services. He led the company through a period of time, and investment, that fundamentally changed the way IBM did business, the message it delivered to its customers, and the way the market perceived the transformed company.

In 2000, IBM posted its sixth straight year of record revenue: $88.4 billion, with earnings of $8.1 billion, a 16 percent increase from the year before. Since 1992, IBM's stock price had gone up nearly 800 percent; its investment potential had increased almost 70 percent from its 1993 low.

By 2001, services represented 40 percent of IBM's pretax income; it's the fastest growing part of IBM in a marketplace where services represent 60 percent of spending. Eighty percent of IBM's target audience were able to identify e-business—a term IBM coined; they associated IBM with e-business four times more often than rivals such as Microsoft.

Not everything is perfect at IBM. By 2001, along with the rest of the national economy, IBM's fortunes dipped. The company posted its first decline in annual revenue since 1993 in December of that year; revenues continued to decline, albeit more slowly, in 2002.

In addition, the market's perception of management and IBM's investment potential still has not caught up to IBM's overall reputation, leaving challenges for current Chairman and CEO Samuel J. Palmisano and his team. Naysayers still call for breaking up the brand, per former CEO John Akers's plan. Rivals Dell, Hewlett-Packard, Sun, and others are spending money and streamlining operations to catch up.

But IBM is not resting on its laurels. It continues to become more wired, faster, leaner, and smarter.

Maureen McGuire describes the future of the company simply: "We are building relationships where we can really add value and bring solutions to bear . . . Those are the things we're trying to do."

Abby Kohnstamm, IBM's chief architect of e-business marketing, has said, "There isn't a company in the world today that doesn't realize that this is an enormous transformation of the way the world runs. We feel that the work we did defined the category, explained the opportunity, and gave us mind-share lead. And that gives us credibility to talk about the future."

Notes

International Business Machines Corporation, Hoover's Online, www. hoovers.com.

Interview with Maureen McGuire, by Jim Gregory, June 13, 2001.

J. G. Auerbach, "IBM Sees Problems Easing Later in Year," *Wall Street Journal*, May 10, 2000.

W. M. Bulkeley, "Infrastructure Sexy? IBM Ads Try to Make It So," *Wall Street Journal*, Dec. 12, 2000.

T. Elkin, "Branding Big Blue," *Advertising Age*, Feb. 28, 2000.

G. Farrell, "Building a New Big Blue," *USA Today*, Nov. 22, 1999.

L. Gerstner, Chairman's Foreword, 2000 IBM Annual Report.

L. Gerstner, Conversation with Lou Dobbs, CNN, May 17, 2001.

L. Gerstner, Speech, Comdex '95, Las Vegas, NV.

D. Kirkpatrick, "IBM: from Big Blue Dinosaur to E-Business Animal," *Fortune*, April 26, 1999.

K. Kranhold, "Big Blue Aims to Distance Itself from Rivals in Web Consulting," *Wall Street Journal*, April 6, 2000.

J. Markoff, "IBM Plans a Campaign to Give Its Image a Boost," *New York Times*, Dec. 31, 1992.

Samuel J. Palmisano, Chairman's Letter, IBM Annual Report 2002.

G. Rifkin, "The Media Business: Magazine Ads Push Computer Commercials Out of the Picture," *New York Times*, Oct. 19, 1992.

I. Sager, "Big Blue Gets Wired," *BusinessWeek*, April 3, 2000.

Chapter Seventeen	# Best Practice No. 10

**Know How to Choose
Your Next CEO**

Being a CEO these days isn't what it used to be. Far from being the corporate superstars of the 1990s, lauded as much on talk shows as in the business press, corporate leaders are increasingly under intense scrutiny from the media, from regulators, politicians, and, not least, shareholders.

In part, this is due to the economic stress that began in 2001, as the stock market collapsed and new economy companies got wiped out. In part, it is due to the increasing spread of corporate and CEO scandals.

CEO candidates are in short supply, even as turnover at the highest levels occurs at startling rates. According to outplacement firm Challenger, Gray & Christmas, there were 473 CEO departures from major U.S. firms in the first 5 months of 2001 alone. This was a 22 percent increase over the same period the previous year.

Candidates for the top job themselves are wary: They don't want to take the reins of a company headed for trouble. As Jeffrey Garten, dean of the Yale School of Management, told the *Wall Street Journal*, "Anyone who takes a CEO job now has to ask the question of how big is the risk [because] . . . From day one, they're "going to be held responsible for the company's performance."

But selecting the right successor to head a corporation is crucial to the company's long-term business success, and the success of the corporate brand. Like so many other important decisions, General Electric (GE) knew how to handle its corporate succession correctly—choosing a leader who would take the torch from Jack Welch and continue to lead the company to even greater heights.

> *I'm a complete and utter zealot for this company.*
> —Jeff Immelt, Chairman and CEO, GE

GENERAL ELECTRIC
THE SUCCESSION

Thanksgiving weekend, 2000, Jack Welch boarded a GE corporate jet in Palm Beach, Florida. He was on a super-secret, cross-country mission to tell two runners-up that they had not won the prize of succeeding Welch as the CEO of General Electric.

That honor went to Jeffrey R. Immelt, head of GE's medical systems business, and a veteran of the company for almost 20 years. Jeff Immelt had big shoes to fill. He knew it; the world knew it. The question is, how did the leadership transition affect the brand . . . and how did GE prepare for the inevitable change of command?

The search for a successor to Jack Welch began in 1994, at the June meeting of the GE board's Management Development and Compensation Committee (MDCC). The group discussed 24 candidates, all of them GE insiders. *Fortune* reporter Geoffrey Colvin wrote that GE "broke most of . . . the rules for corporate succession planning. They never named [an] . . . heir apparent. They never looked at an outsider."

An internal GE succession was an important part of Welch's vision for the company's future. In 1999, Welch told the *Wall Street Journal* that shared values are one of the key secrets to successful management.

"If your business values are different," Welch said, "if your treatment of people is different, if you don't agree about the behavior you want to cultivate in your company, that is a problem."

From 1994 on, Welch and the board kept a sharp eye on all the candidates, spending thousands of hours interacting with each of them in meetings, presentations, conferences, and retreats. The candidates' progress was reviewed twice a year at the annual board and MDCC meetings. Each time, Welch gave his assessment, and board members shared their opinions based on the numerous exchanges and experiences each had had with the various candidates. According to Welch, the key part of the selection process was "all chemistry, blood, sweat, family, feelings."

In June 2000, Welch named the top three finalists, all from the original pool of 24. But before the succession was finalized, GE announced that it was acquiring Honeywell—its biggest acquisition to date—for $45 billion in stock. Welch announced that he would stay at GE a few months longer than planned, but that his successor would take over in late 2001.

In the end, the Honeywell deal derailed, and the transition sped up: Welch announced Immelt's promotion in late November 2000. Despite the problems created by the Honeywell venture, *Fortune* called the transition "one of the best orchestrated [corporate] successions in history."

Welch's last day on the job was Friday, September 7, 2001. Immelt's first day on the job was Monday, September 10.

The next day, terrorists attacked the World Trade Center. Two GE employees were killed. The company took a $600 million hit to its insurance business, and its aircraft engine business slowed immediately. GE's stock dropped almost 11 percent when the New York Stock Exchange reopened 6 days after the attacks.

Not long afterwards, anthrax was found at GE-owned NBC, and Enron imploded, exposing GE to the tune of $80 million. At the same time, a rash of corporate scandals, from Tyco to WorldCom, punctured investor and consumer trust in America's largest corporations.

Jack Welch had enjoyed almost unlimited investor confidence— but Jack Welch never had to deal with the environment that greeted Immelt from his second day on the job. Beyond the general environment, investors' faith in GE was further shaken by the idea that there was a new man at the helm.

Shored up by his own belief in the strength of GE, Immelt's strategy was to open up the company to unprecedented scrutiny and to communicate with key constituencies in new and powerful ways.

Responding to speculation about "what would Jack do," Immelt replied, "If Jack were here, he would be talking about doing different things. We have different styles, and we communicate different ways. But he was about doing what worked best . . . That's what I'm about."

Richard Costello, Manager of Corporate Marketing Communications, told us how the new business environment affected the company's communications decisions.

"September 11th happened," Costello says. "I think a decade ago we would probably have taken some time off the air and then come back on, business as usual. What we decided to do was get back as quickly as we could, and we developed advertising tuned to the moment—about rolling up your sleeves; getting back to work, America; and so on.

"One of our first print ads out there was of the Statue of Liberty rolling up her sleeves," Costello continues. "There was a certain amount of controversy inside the company: Should we be playing around with the Statue of Liberty? But it really hit a chord. We got tremendous response from both our employees and some very important customers. We sell to the Defense Department; we sell to the Marines, the Air Force—the Marine Corps asked for copies of the ad for all of their people.

"If you walk around GE, you hear from our salespeople that they hand it out to customers; it's still around. That ad ran once in every newspaper, on the Friday afterward, but the amount of comment we got on it and the amount of legs it's had are quite extraordinary. It was the right thing to do at that moment: We reacted quickly, and we captured something that people felt good about. And particularly when you're selling a big icon, that's part of what it's all about."

GE's CoreBrand Power clearly reflects the changes the company was experiencing. Its score began faltering when investors became aware that Jack Welch was facing mandatory retirement. After a peak in 1996, the company's CoreBrand Power began to decline; by 2001, with a CoreBrand Power of 69, GE's rating had slipped 16 percent in a 5-year period.

Even so, in 2001 the company's CoreBrand Power was higher than its peer set, although this was largely driven by familiarity. Perceptions of GE's management and investment potential did not outpace its nearest competitors; despite annual earnings growth, perceptions did not improve in the years immediately before the transition. Clearly, the end of Welch's 20 years of powerhouse management was making investors wary. You can see the progression of GE's Core-Brand Power scores in Figures 17-1 through 17-5.

Richard Costello explains the shifts in CoreBrand Power: "The failure of the Honeywell deal and the transition hurt us. We did great when Jack was at the peak of his reputation, in the mid-1990s, and the market was booming. As the market softened and as Jack was ending his career as CEO, we had a miscue on the buy of Honeywell and confused the market by that kind of unexpected action.

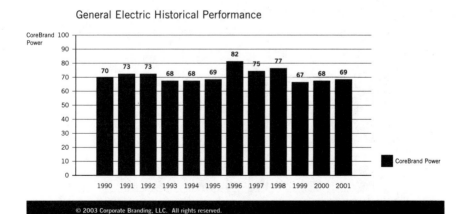

Figure 17-1. CoreBrand Power 1990–2001, General Electric Historical Performance

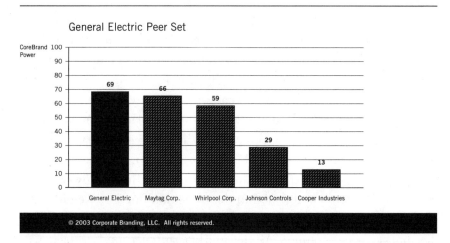

Figure 17-2. CoreBrand Power 2001, General Electric Partial Peer Set

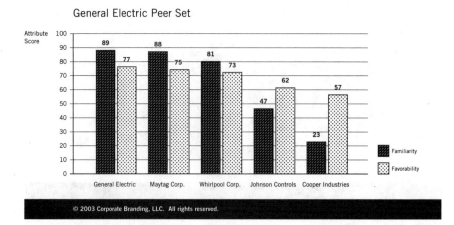

Figure 17-3. Familiarity and Favorability 2001, General Electric Partial Peer Set

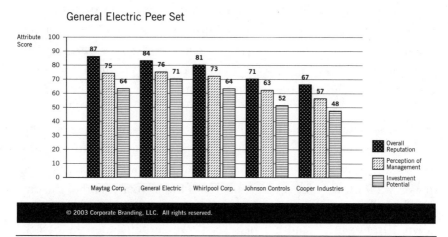

Favorability Attributes 2001

General Electric Peer Set

Figure 17-4. Favorability Attributes 2001, General Electric Partial Peer Set

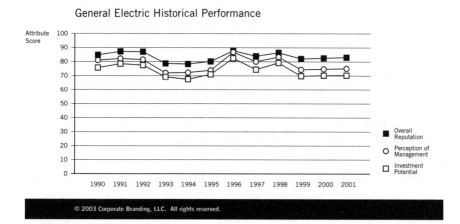

Favorability Attributes 1990 - 2001

General Electric Historical Performance

Figure 17-5. Favorability Attributes 1990–2001, General Electric Historical Performance

After the tragedies of late 2001, Immelt began to stabilize operations. The shareholders' statement for first quarter 2002 showed a 17
percent earnings increase (before an accounting change).

Despite that positive news, shares sank 9.3 percent on the day of
the release. Costello underscores the difference that perception of new
management can make: "The press releases for our earnings for the
first quarter in 2002 and 2001 were so close in language, performance, everything—and the market response was literally in opposite
directions.

"I was down in Washington when I saw the first quarter 2002
release come out on the newswire," Costello recalls. "I read it, and it
was great, exactly what we said we would do. I put it away; nothing
to worry about, we'd be up one and a half bucks by the end of the day.

"I got home that night and looked at the stock price, and we were
down 10 percent. I couldn't believe it. We actually met the Street's
expectations on operating performance and earnings, and we still lost
10 percent."

Immelt used the media to send a reassuring message to GE
employees—not coincidentally the largest group of shareholders of
GE stock.

"Between September 11th, Enron, and the downturn in the economy, there's a whole variety of environmental issues that have been
punishing our stock," Costello told us. "And our employees were getting agitated about it. I mean, they're our single biggest block of
shareholders. And so, Jeff's point was, we've got to talk about it.

"Jeff felt that we needed a public stance," Costello continues. "So
we developed some print ads, which we knocked out literally in a couple of days, and ran them in the *Wall Street Journal*, the *New York
Times*, and the local newspapers in the markets where we've got high
concentrations of employees.

"We got a positive response back from that. We're trying to reas-
sure both the market and the people we're around that we're in this
for the long run."

In the April 2002 Annual Report to Share Owners, Immelt told his
audience, "GE is a company with an under-performing share price.

To be specific, since I became Chairman it's dropped more than 15%. I hate where our stock price is today. Our stock price doesn't reflect the performance of this company or our value. . . .

"The U.S. industrial economy has declined throughout 2001," he continued. "Europe is slow while Japan is in recession. The tragedy of 9/11 had a specific impact on our airline and insurance customers. But we did what we said we're going to do: Grow earnings and cash flow by double digits."

In this, Immelt was fulfilling the expectations GE has developed and delivered on for years, of a minimum 10 percent profit growth. In the Welch years, that growth equaled steady increases in the stock price, an equation Immelt has had a hard time duplicating.

Immelt's reputation as a star performer within GE—and as Welch's handpicked successor—is a critical component of his ability to lead the company and to soothe investors over time. An outsider new to the colossal job of running GE wouldn't have the familiarity with GE's businesses, and with Welch's methods, nor would they have the internal track record or relationships that won Immelt his position.

Immelt is nothing if not a GE man . . . in fact, he is "second-generation" GE, since his father spent 38 years with GE's Aircraft Engines. After a stint at Procter & Gamble and earning an MBA from Harvard Business School, the younger Immelt went to GE headquarters as a marketing exec in 1982.

Immelt got Welch's attention in 1989, when—following a series of tough negotiations—he persuaded client GM to increase its billings with GE. For the next decade, Immelt moved through the management ranks, becoming head of GE's medical systems division before being tapped as the next CEO.

Outside the company, it's hard to remember that Immelt's famous predecessor also had a rough start when he became CEO in 1981. The economy was stumbling, Japanese industry and technology were providing furious competition, and there were critics who expected that Welch would have to split up GE.

"There are all kinds of tough periods," Welch told *BusinessWeek*. "He [Immelt] has got better results than I had."

JEFF IMMELT'S PLAN FOR GROWTH

Immelt's plans for a "twenty-first-century GE" focuses on four areas that will add value to shareholders. They represent a mix between Welch's company-wide initiatives and Immelt's own priorities for the future.

1. **Invest in product superiority:** Launch more Six Sigma-designed products, enter high potential areas like molecular imaging and distributed energy, and modernize the GE Global Research Center.
2. **Grow services:** Continue to develop this area, which grew 13 percent in 2001.
3. **Intensify globalization:** Build non-U.S. sales, especially in Europe and China.
4. **Expand capability:** Acquire companies that offer GE new areas for growth.

Immelt is building on the lessons he learned from Welch, while positioning GE for future growth. Like the "Neutron Jack" of the 1980s, Immelt plans to reduce staff, targeting the 40 percent of employees who are in administration and support. He plans to build on the Six Sigma quality program, continue Welch's expansion into global markets, and maintain an aggressive schedule of acquisitions.

But Immelt also plans to make his own mark. In a departure from Welch, Immelt will tie managers' performance to customers' business growth; he is also mandating that salespeople increase the amount of time they spend with customers—from 30 percent to up to 80 percent of the work week.

Immelt is also changing the face of GE, literally, by demanding diversity both in top management and throughout the ranks. In 2001, GE's 31 top executives were all male; 30 were white. That balance is changing: More recently, half of all new senior executives and new corporate officers have been women, minorities, or employees from outside the United States.

Immelt's management is winning points with those whom—in the short term—it may count the most: GE employees. In March 2002, an internal GE survey of 75,000 employees—expanded from 15,000 the year before—showed that more than 80 percent of respondents expressed confidence in their new leader and approved his enthusiasm and vision. But it's not all "Mr. Nice Guy." Employees know they have to work hard to meet Immelt's expectations of reduced "backroom" time and a lot more customer interaction.

Immelt is quick to acknowledge his role as custodian and champion of the house that Edison built. In his address to shareholders in April 2002, he reminded his listeners that GE has "been part of the progress of the U.S. economy for the last 120 years."

He also acknowledges his debt to Jack Welch, while underscoring the different qualities that they offer. As Immelt told *BusinessWeek*, "Every day at GE, I had bosses—including Jack—who were always there to help me find the right answers. A bad boss is there to trip you up, or find the wrong answer. Jack created at GE the spirit of finding the right answer, finding the right way.

"Jack and I are different people, and we go about our work in different ways. But I did learn from Jack that a CEO really has three jobs. One is to perform, two is to create the future, and three is never let anybody else define who you are."

At the same time, Immelt realizes that the field is his—with luck, for another 20-plus years. He described his new team as being "customer-oriented. They'll be technology-savvy. They're all going to share the traits of where I want to take the company. Will the people in the future be different ones than Jack would have picked? Absolutely.

"People say, 'Oh God, Jack is gone. What now?' You've got people throughout this company who think it's about us now. We think we can grow it. We think we can make it successful."

Richard Costello agrees. Immelt, he says, "is young, straightforward, honest, a regular sort of a guy. When you see him on TV, he comes across in some ways as much more likeable than Jack.

"I really think now we're struggling with the environmental thing; we're still struggling with an attitude of—'show me, Jeff.' The master is gone—show us. And I think he will. In my mind there is absolutely no doubt."

Notes

"Higher CEO Turnover," The Chief Executive, London School of Economics, http://www.bestofbiz.com/briefings/default.asp?p=193.

"Jeff Immelt's 2002 Annual Report to Share Owners," Waukesha, Wisconsin, April 24, 2002, http://www.ge.com/news/dwnlds/2002_AddressToShareOwners.pdf.

Interview with Richard Costello, General Electric, by Jim Gregory, May 1, 2002.

Diane Brady, "GE's Jeff Immelt: His Own Man," *BusinessWeek* Online, Sept. 17, 2001, http://netscape.businessweek.com/magazine/content/01_38/b3749088.htm.

Diane Brady, "Q&A with GE's Jeff Immelt," *BusinessWeek* Online, April 29, 2002, http://www.businessweek.com/magazine/content/02_17/b3780007.htm.

Diane Brady, "The Education of Jeff Immelt," *BusinessWeek* Online, April 29, 2002, http://www.businessweek.com/magazine/content/02_17/b3780001.htm.

Geoffrey Colvin, "Changing of the Guard," *Fortune*, Jan. 8, 2001.

Justin Fox, "What About Jeff?" *Fortune*, June 24, 2002, http://www.fortune.com/indexw.jhtml?channel=artcol.jhtml&doc_id=208333.

Carol Hymowitz and Matt Murray, "Raises or Praises or Out the Door," *Wall Street Journal*, June 21, 1999.

Letter to Shareholders, GE 2000 Annual Report, Feb. 9, 2001.

Joann S. Lublin and Carol Hymowitz, "Fearing Scandals, Executives Spurn CEO Job Offers," *Wall Street Journal*, June 27, 2002.

Anna Torrance and Alistair Craven, "Tales from the Top—the Contrasting Styles of Today's CEOs," *Management First*, http://www.managementfirst.com/articles/ceo.htm.

Chapter Eighteen | **Best Practice No. 11**

Treasure Your Employees

Virtually every large company will say that it values its employees, but very few actually put their employees first.

Southwest Airlines is one of those companies: Empowered employees are the engine that drives its business. Since the company's rough and tumble beginnings, Southwest has acted on the principle that happy employees create happy customers—and that profits will quickly follow.

From sharing profits to painting employee names on the hulls of its aircraft, Southwest goes all out to show employees that they're number one.

This attitude has created an enviable company culture that's been carefully nurtured for the past 31 years . . . and has made Southwest the airline to beat.

> *The Golden Rule is the basis for everything.*
> —Joyce Rogge,
> Senior Vice President, Marketing,
> Southwest Airlines

SOUTHWEST AIRLINES
NURTURING THEIR NO. 1 ASSET

The year was 1967. In sleepy San Antonio, Texas, Colleen C. Barrett took a job as a legal secretary. Too poor to afford law school, Colleen loved the law and thought she had found her life's work. Her boss was a guy named Herb Kelleher, and before long, he would change Colleen's life—and just about everybody else's.

Today, Colleen Barrett is President, Chief Operating Officer, and "Queen of Hearts" of Southwest Airlines, the company Herb founded with Rollin King in 1967 as Air Southwest.

The Southwest promise is built on two pillars: low cost and outstanding service. The strategy has paid off handsomely: Southwest has delivered profits for 29 consecutive years. Kelleher, in his years at the helm, proved to be a consummate leader, sharing the rewards of success and motivating his staff to meet and beat the challenges they faced with hard work, good humor, and a strong team spirit.

In 2001, Kelleher stepped back from his role as President and CEO, although he remains Chairman of the Board. He was succeeded by his long-time lieutenants: Southwest veterans James F. (Jim) Parker, former corporate counsel, and Colleen Barrett. While Jim, as Vice Chairman and CEO, is the company's official outside spokesman, it is Barrett who is the keeper of the company culture . . . and its brand identity.

The famous Southwest company culture is shaped by the airline's earliest experiences fighting for the right to exist. Four years of lawsuits followed the company's inception. Rollin, Herb, and first President Lamar Muse did whatever it took to get their airline running and infused that fighting spirit into their employees for the next 3 decades.

Joyce Rogge, Southwest's Senior Vice President of Marketing, told us, "Back in the initial days when it was such a battle to get our first planes off the ground, a very strong culture emerged. We had a lot of young, feisty employees, and there was just a belief that they could make this work. They didn't know if they were going to get a paycheck, but they were sure going to make this work.

"So there was an immediate family feeling back when there were 100 people trying to make this thing happen," Rogge continues. "And that family feeling never got lost."

The company's dedication to its employees is enshrined in its mission statement, which hasn't varied since it was first written. As Joyce Rogge points out, "The very first thing the mission statement talks about is how we're going to treat our employees, how we're going to care for our employees. And after that it talks about what we're going to do for our customers."

Tim McClure, one of the founders of Southwest's long-term agency GSD&M, observes, "The thing here that shocks everybody is that the customer does not come first, the employees come first. The point of view is that if the employees are treated well and are happy, then the customer will be treated well and be happy.

"That's counter to all teachings I've ever heard about how to run a company," McClure continues. "It's always, the customer is always right. Our point of view is, the customer is not always right. They're

---

SOUTHWEST'S MISSION STATEMENT

Southwest Airlines' mission statement is short, sweet, and to the point. Here it is, in its entirety.

THE MISSION OF SOUTHWEST AIRLINES

The mission of Southwest Airlines is dedication to the highest quality of Customer Service delivered with a sense of warmth, friendliness, individual pride, and Company Spirit.

TO OUR EMPLOYEES

We are committed to provide our Employees a stable work environment with equal opportunity for learning and personal growth. Creativity and innovation are encouraged for improving the effectiveness of Southwest Airlines. Above all, Employees will be provided the same concern, respect, and caring attitude within the Organization that they are expected to share externally with every Southwest Customer.

always a customer, and we hope they're going to be happy, but it starts with our people."

From the beginning, employees were encouraged to think like owners: Management allowed workers to do what they needed to do to get the job done, without micromanaging. In return, Southwest's employees made their company the best in the business, with personable customer service, a strong on-time record and that famous profitability.

"Herb has always said, and Jim Parker now says, that we're not in this to lose money," Joyce Rogge says. "So the goal of profitability is part of our fabric.

"Everybody who works here knows our goal," she continues. "From administrative assistants to the guys that work on the ramp, they all understand about keeping costs low, so that we can charge low fares, so that we can make money. It's all wrapped up."

Keeping the company culture strong and employee motivation high is where Colleen Barrett shows her special genius. Tim McClure says that Barrett worked with the agency to develop "something unheard of at the time"—a planned, strategic corporate culture.

Barrett nurtures and creates the culture through actions large and small, personal and systemwide. Barrett created the training programs that teach staff how to interact with customers through Southwest's trademark humorous, informal approach. She personally greets many new hires and takes the time to write notes recognizing milestones in employees' lives.

McClure observes, "This culture thing is no different than a marriage. If you work at it every day it will work; if you don't, it will fail. Colleen is like the culture chiropractor: She keeps it in alignment."

Rogge says, "We used to have other companies come in and study us, because they wanted to try to replicate our culture. One of the things we would tell them is, it's not about having birthday celebrations. That's part of it, but you can't just say, we're going to wear casual clothes and have birthday celebrations. If the company is not really and truly putting its employees first, then all the celebrations in the world won't fix it."

Employees are even an important factor in judging the company's advertising. Joyce Rogge says, "The first audience for our advertising is our own employees. We ask ourselves, is it motivating? Is it exciting them? Is it making them proud?

"We've had customer feedback where we haven't necessarily changed what we're doing," Rogge reveals. "But when we get employee feedback on something they don't like, we often make a change, because it isn't worth it. Even when we know the ad is doing a good job, if it's not doing well for the employees then it doesn't matter."

Richard Sweet, Southwest's Senior Director of Marketing and Sales, adds that the ads aren't worth much if employees aren't behind the message. "They have to believe in the message to deliver it," Sweet says. "And they're the ones that deliver it."

As a rapidly growing business, Southwest has met the challenge of adding new members to the team by making its hiring process a key part of its strategy.

The mission of the People Department—Southwest's significantly simple name for its human resources group—is to keep Southwest a fun place to work. As Tim McClure says, "We look for people that like to color outside the lines, to bend the rules."

According to Colleen Barrett, "The company is based on people, and that means if you hire right you get on the right track. We hire for attitude—for personality—not for industry qualifications or experience."

The interview process is unusual, to say the least. Richard Sweet explains, "For a lot of our positions there will be group interviews, to understand people's personalities, and how they interact with people.

"We probably learn as much about an applicant before the interview as we do during it," Sweet told us, "because we watch them interact with other job candidates. We see people that are introverted, people that are self-important, but the people that just love people make it through the initial interview. They have to tell something funny about themselves. And then we have them work together in groups of two or three to come up with a solution to some kind of customer service problem."

Sweet cautions that "this culture isn't for everybody. If you envision yourself wearing a suit and being recognized as important, you may be uncomfortable in this place."

The process works both ways, allowing prospects to interact with the company and see if there's a personality fit even before a job is offered.

Joyce Rogge says, "Many times, when people start working here, they say, 'I've found where I belong.'

"We have an award that we give out at our annual marketing meeting," Rogge continues. "It's called the Boomerang Award, because it's for people that leave and come back. They may have been making 50 percent more salary, but as one woman said, 'Where were the balloons? Nobody came by and asked me to have lunch; the people just weren't nice.' And it's not that they weren't 'nice,' they just didn't work in an environment where that was expected.

"We hire the kind of people, who, if you're having a birthday, they're going to make sure they say, happy birthday," Rogge continues. "If your mother is ill, they're going to find out how she's doing. The Golden Rule is the basis for everything. If you aren't a person who's going to treat people the way you want to be treated, then it isn't going to work."

The success of the company's culture in building the brand is reflected in its CoreBrand Power. In 2001, Southwest's CoreBrand Power was 45. Not a high rating in general terms, but the second highest among its peer group in the airline industry and significantly higher than such long-haul giants as United Airlines and American Airlines.

More importantly, perhaps, Southwest's favorability rating is the highest among its peer set. When we look more deeply at the favorability attributes, we see that Southwest's score is driven by a high perception of management and investment potential. You can see how Southwest's CoreBrand Power compares to its peers in Figures 18-1, 18-2, and 18-3.

Between 1990 and 1996, Southwest enjoyed an unbroken upward trajectory in its CoreBrand Power scores. But in 1997, Southwest's CoreBrand Power dropped sharply, largely in response to perceived management issues. Figures 18-4, 18-5, and 18-6 show the com-

CoreBrand Power 2001

Southwest Airlines Peer Set

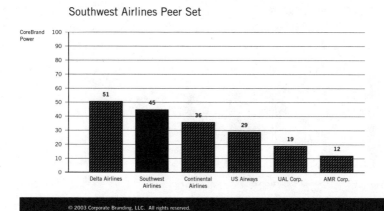

Figure 18-1. CoreBrand Power 2001, Southwest Airlines Peer Set

Familiarity and Favorability 2001

Southwest Airlines Peer Set

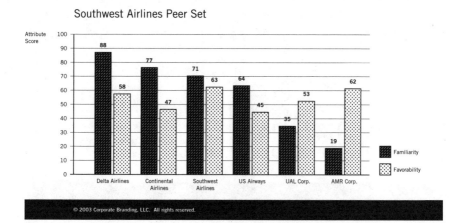

Figure 18-2. Familiarity and Favorability 2001, Southwest Airlines Peer Set

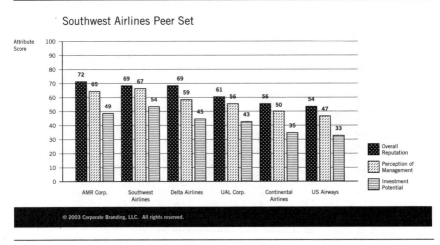

Figure 18-3. Favorability Attributes 2001, Southwest Airlines Peer Set

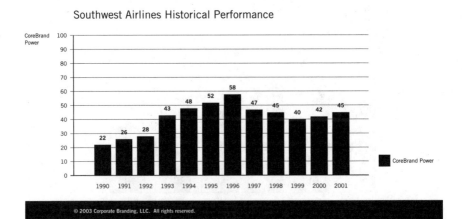

Figure 18-4. CoreBrand Power 1990–2001, Southwest Airlines Historical
Performance

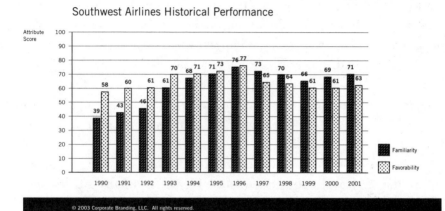

Figure 18-5. Familiarity and Favorability 1990–2001, Southwest Airlines Historical Performance

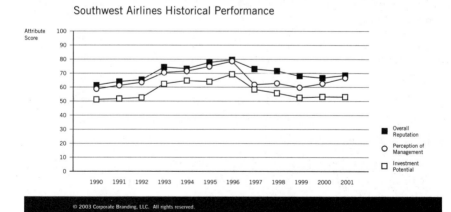

Figure 18-6. Favorability Attributes 1990–2001, Southwest Airlines Historical Performance

pany's historical CoreBrand Power performance between 1990 and 2001.

As Tim McClure recounts, "That was a point where the analyst world was asking what comes after Herb. Herb had built a clear succession plan, but he wasn't sharing it. He was in his mid-60s, and nobody knew what was going to happen when he retired.

"You also had some airlines going out of business then," McClure continues. "There were a lot of people saying that this was the perfect time for Southwest to merge, or be bought. So I think the sharp drop in 1997 also had a lot to do with the perceived uncertainty about where the airline was going."

Like the rest of its industry, Southwest faces a more complex future for air travel. After September 11, the company stuck to its principles of supporting its staff and serving the customer.

Tim McClure says, "After 9/11, they didn't pull back any flights, and they didn't lay off any people. By philosophy, they didn't feel like that was the thing to do. Within 2 weeks, it was business as usual: They didn't cut back flights, they didn't reduce service, they didn't fire anybody. In fact, they had signs saying, 'we're hiring.' And people said, 'This is different; this is not the experience I had elsewhere.' "

As the climate for air travel continues to evolve, Southwest continues to approach new challenges with both optimism and that ever-present eye on the customer.

Joyce Rogge says, "Our big focus for the short term is giving customers at the airport an easier, faster, more pleasant experience. We're going to introduce automated processes that we've resisted in the past, because we're so cost-efficient. But now there are so many things that are hassles for the customer, that the things we can control we're going to make easier."

Tim McClure adds, "When we did our research on this airline, the first thing we found out is that people think of Southwest differently than other airlines.

"Southwest may well become the largest airline in America in the next 5 years, because what they do works."

Notes

Interview with Joyce Rogge, Senior Vice President, Marketing, Southwest Airlines, by Jim Gregory, May 23, 2002.

Interview with Richard Sweet, Senior Director, Marketing and Sales, Southwest Airlines, by Jim Gregory, May 23, 2002.

Interview with Tim McClure, founder, GSD&M, by Jim Gregory, May 23, 2002.

Quarterly Financials, Southwest Airlines Co., Hoover's Online, www.hoovers.com.

Southwest Airlines Co., Hoover's Online, www.hoovers.com.

Southwest Fact Sheet, Revised April 18, 2002, Southwest Airlines.

"The Mission of Southwest Airlines," Southwest Airlines, www.southwest.com.

Margaret Allen, "Ground Controller," *Dallas Business Journal*, Aug. 3–9, 2001.

David Field, "Southwest Succession," *Airline Business*, April 2002.

K. Freiberg and J. Freiberg, *Nuts*, Bard Press, Austin, TX, 1996.

Jonathan R. Laing, "Nothing but Blue Skies," *Barron's*, July 2, 2001.

Chapter Nineteen

Best Practice No. 12

Build a Brand on a Budget

Building a brand is a process . . . meaning that both money and time can be spent in increments, if necessary, to achieve your goals.

Air Products and Chemicals, Inc., was built over time in a typical "silo" fashion. Multiple groups of businesses operated independently, with separate streams of communications, responsibilities, and reporting. Input to headquarters took place only at the leadership level. Air Products was the equivalent of a holding company with multiple businesses in the Americas, Asia, and Europe—its business unit had as little to do with one another culturally as they did geographically.

But the idea of branding is a powerful force. Slowly, using the leverage of internal communications—before a cent was ever spent on external communications—Air Products came into its own as a global brand.

> *Our customers know that they can sleep at night if they deal with us.*
>
> —John Dodds,
> Global Marketing Communications Director,
> Air Products

AIR PRODUCTS
DELIVERING THE DIFFERENCE

Air Products & Chemicals is an international supplier of industrial gases, chemicals, and related equipment. The company was founded over 60 years ago in the back of a Detroit mortuary. Today, head-quartered in Allentown, Pennsylvania, it has 18,000 employees in over 30 countries and $5.7 billion in annual revenue. Its customer base includes NASA, as well as companies in steel and oil production, chemicals processing, healthcare, and electronics manufacturing.

For many years, Air Products was known as a gases and chemicals company. But according to John Dodds, Air Products' Global Marketing Communications Director, "As we moved into new areas like medical and services we needed to have a much wider remit for our brand; it had to be understood by a lot more people."

"Our company has changed," Dodds continues. "It's become more global. Our portfolio of offerings has changed from delivering not only gases and chemicals, but offering, in addition, services and solutions. We are leaders in our marketplaces, but the world didn't know about us. We had to unify our brand with a single differentiator around the world for all of our businesses."

Air Products' CoreBrand Power clearly illustrates Dodds's assertion that "the world didn't know" the company. Among its peer set, Air Products was among the least well known, with a tiny score of 12. Among the people who knew the company, however, it was well liked; its favorability score of 57 was in line with or better than many of its competitors. A comparison of Air Products' CoreBrand Power with its peers is shown in Figures 19-1 and 19-2.

Dodds's goal was to "attain a true leadership position with our brand in our marketplace." But Air Products had a problem. Their business units—and budgets—were fragmented geographically and along organizational lines. Each individual business unit put the success of its own product lines above the overall corporate brand. As Dodds remarked, "We had lots of smaller budgets, with lots of small amounts of money."

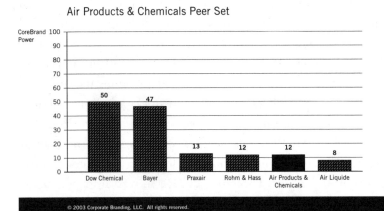

Figure 19-1. CoreBrand Power 2001, Air Products Peer Set

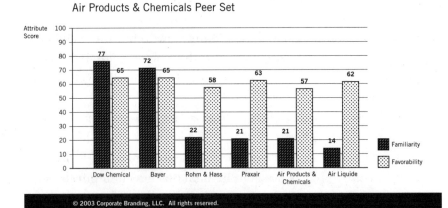

Figure 19-2. Familiarity and Favorability 2001, Air Products Peer Set

Air Products' corporate communications department didn't have the budget to develop the corporate brand—but an opportunity to begin the process surfaced when one of the company's divisions approached corporate for some communications help.

Cecil Chappelow and Colin Smith, the U.S. and European heads of Air Products' Global Applications Division at the time, wanted to boost their division's market recognition. Dodds characterizes their group as "the development and knowledge base of our company." As a first step, the company employed branding consultancy Interbrand in Europe to undertake a research and positioning exercise, which yielded two key perceptions. First, the companies surveyed felt strongly that Air Products had a deeper understanding of their businesses than many of its competitors. There was also agreement that Air Products' employees were smart people who had the understanding, integrity, and passion to succeed in their complicated field.

As Dodds told us, the research showed that "Our clients didn't think we were always the cheapest option, but at the end of the day they knew that they could rely on us, that they could sleep at night if they dealt with us, and that's money in the bank. In many cases, we have people working inside the customers' facilities, providing a sense of dependability and trustworthiness that they don't get from anyone else."

For a company that had always focused its communications on products, this was an exciting discovery. Dodds then took the process a step further. He put together a project team that included Air Products management in the United States and Europe, together with the company's U.S. and European advertising agencies: Interbrand, Carton Donofrio Partners, and Ogilvy Primary Contact. The team identified three brand values based on the research: "Understanding, Integrity, and Passion."

Next on the agenda was to develop a brand positioning statement which focused on Air Products' employees: "Our strength is our great people . . . As a result, we create lasting relationships, always built on understanding."

At this point, the company had limited its investment to research, and developing the brand definition that the research suggested.

Before taking the process any further, Dodds and his colleagues shopped the new idea around the company, talking to executives and business managers around the world about the new branding concept.

"The whole concept—even just the word 'branding'—for industrial companies is quite a difficult one," Dodds told us. "Branding is a word that many people felt was related more to Coca-Cola than an industrial gas company. There was a view that it was not really essential."

But eventually, senior management started buying into the concept, especially when they learned that communications would most likely feature Air Products' people as its strength . . . and that this could be successfully leveraged through regional communications programs.

The momentum of the branding project was temporarily derailed by a failed acquisition attempt by Air Products and Air Liquide of BOC. But when the deal fell through, the company found itself in a new ball game. As Dodds describes it, "Confidence with employees was dented, and we needed a springboard."

"But what we did have was a visionary new Chairman and CEO with a new set of strategies, who supported the brand positioning internally and externally," Dodds continues. "We had a brand that had been validated and ready to go. And that gave us a very strong position to be able to push the button. Timing is everything. We were able to convince the most senior people that branding the company was the right move, and we moved ahead quite quickly after the BOC deal fell through."

The branding initiative was introduced first to employees. The emphasis was on creating a new worldwide culture for the company, unified under one brand identity. The brand statement and values were used to create a series of guidelines affecting communications, media relations, and even employee behaviors. Internal communications featured employees from every corner of the world. Even though the core messages were the same for every unit, the language was changed slightly to reflect local sensibilities.

When it came to external communications, the brand helped the company realize greater efficiencies as well as greater recognition. Where the company previously had fragmented and inefficient communications in each of their markets, Air Products began to introduce branded communications that could be localized for every region and tangibly support local programs.

Dodds says, "Today we have a global look and feel, as well as a global set of processes for our communications, which means that ads can run in local languages in Europe and Asia, just the way they run in the United States. Historically that was difficult to do, with different regional managers having different perspectives."

Dodds continues, "Before the branding effort, the business units never had the luxury of an umbrella brand to support them, and they had to do all the work selling our products and our company themselves. Once there was a brand that was actually promoting our company, as well as featuring our products, they felt much happier. And they were quite happy to have a new look and feel for their communications, because now there was something to act as the driver to communicate their business differentiators."

Chairman and CEO John Jones called that driver "Deliver the Difference," a combination of core strategies, values, and a vision to take the company forward.

"Deliver the difference," Dodds says, "is literally the corporate blueprint that maps how our people around the world will keep delivering the Air Products difference in the marketplace." That message is steered to all key stakeholders through the Corporate Communications team.

Air Products keeps its branding expenses low. There is no separate organization to develop and grow the brand. Instead, Dodds and his

---

Chairman, President, and CEO John P. Jones III, in his 2002 Letter to Shareholders, emphasized Air Products' key brand differentiation: "Each and every Air Products employee, each and every day, is looking for ways to do things more efficiently and quickly for our customers." He continued: "The Air Products difference is our people. They're the ones who have created long-lasting relationships based on understanding with our customers."

John Dodds's Rules of "Reality Branding" for Smaller Companies

- Whatever stage of development your business is in, visualize the "dream ticket" of where you want to be, so you can keep moving forward to that goal.

- Think small at first, and have patience. Not many industrial companies have a locker of cash waiting to be spent on branding, so we have to do things incrementally. There's a song by Pete Seeger that goes, "inch by inch, row by row, gonna make this garden grow." That's how we approach it.

- Employees that understand and live the brand are as powerful an influence in the company as senior management.

- Timing is everything.

- Surround yourself with people who want to change the world, not the word. There will always be people who say, "I don't like that word." That can slow down the process. Fill your team with positive people who want to light the candles rather than curse the darkness.

- God is in the details. You have to understand the strategy, but get right down and understand the details as well. Integration of messages, design, tone of voice depends on it.

- Never underestimate the power of a freebie. We recognize employee ideas with really cool Air Products gear. It may sound silly, but people appreciate the thought and the recognition. It encourages them to tell me more.

- Touch the areas of personal involvement in peoples' work lives. Think about changing your security cards, because it isn't a prison card, it's an employee's personal identity card. You can have your message there, and it can look and feel the same as all of your other branded material. Create a feeling that every touch point is being addressed.

- A launch is the beginning, not the end of the journey. The business is changing, people are changing, geographies are changing, and so you've got to keep on with the journey.

- Our favorite: There's no absolute truth.

global marketing communications team are working to infuse the brand into customer communications at every level.

"Colleagues of mine work for companies that have dozens of brand-titled employees working for them," Dodds jokes. "We don't have a single person with a brand title, including myself. So, for all of us, it's about nurturing the brand. The brand needs to be articulated and understood by everyone it touches. Our chairman owns the brand, and we are there to take care of it."

The branding effort has paid off, not just in cost efficiencies, but also in increased levels of business. "We have tangible evidence to show that the approach we've taken has yielded business results," Dodds says.

When it comes to future investing in the brand, Dodds also takes the long view, as he has since the beginning. "We have not strayed away from the core principle," he says, "which is that the understanding and knowledge of our people create tangible value for our customers, which in turn creates lasting relationships.

"Having a strong set of strategies is vital," he continues. "Because having a brand with an essence and a personality is nothing unless you have a strong set of strategies that people in the company understand and can follow. It's the employees who are going to deliver on the key business strategies that we have moving forward, and that is how Deliver the Difference and our brand complement each other so well."

Notes

Chairman John P. Jones' Address to Shareholders, Presented at the annual meeting of shareholders, January 24, 2002, www.airproducts.com/fin/chairmans_address.asp

Interview with John Dodds, Global Marketing Communications Director, Air Products, by Jim Gregory, March 20, 2002.

"Air Products Singapore Secures MEGASYS Total Gas Management Contract," PR Newswire, Hoover's Online, www.hoovers.com.

"Chemical Customer Honors CSX Transportation," Hoovers Online, www.hoovers.com.

Air Products and Chemicals, Inc., Hoover's Online, www.hoovers.com.

| Chapter Twenty | # The Worst of Corporate Branding |

S omeday, in the not-too-distant future, the tremendous economic value that corporate brands contribute to financial success will be understood as a universal law of business.

Until that day comes, there will be senior-level executives who scoff at the value of the brand. Unfortunately for their employees and stockholders, these leaders will risk a catastrophic loss of control of their company's CoreBrand Power—and the resulting loss of value inherent in the brand.

Since we don't live in a perfect world, we have many examples of CEOs who mismanage their corporate brands. It isn't difficult to come up with a list of the worst cases of branding. It's sad, really. It takes years to build a brand—but it can be destroyed in an extremely short time.

Here is the current list.

ENRON

Much has been said about the debacle of Enron. Brands are delicate and can be crushed with dishonesty.

ARTHUR ANDERSEN

Ditto.

CITIGROUP

Whoever made the decision to change the parent company name without investing appropriate dollars in a corporate branding campaign should be ashamed.

A seemingly small change from Citicorp to Citigroup actually cost the company a tremendous amount of CoreBrand Power as well as market value. You can see the changes in CoreBrand Power for yourself in Figures 20-1, 20-2, and 20-3. How simple it would have been to launch a communications campaign and to sustain it for 2 years until all the key constituents knew and understood the new corporate brand.

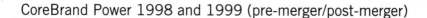

CoreBrand Power 1998 and 1999 (pre-merger/post-merger)

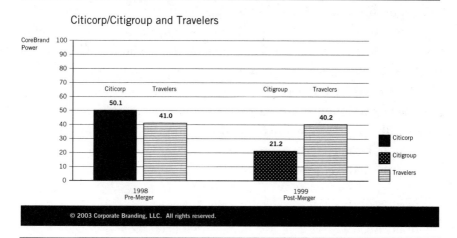

Figure 20-1. CoreBrand Power 1998 and 1999, Citigroup Peer Set

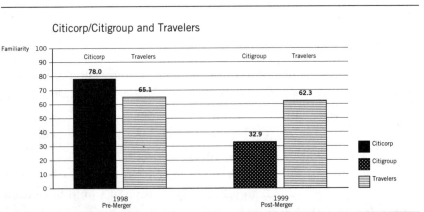

Figure 20-2. Familiarity Attributes 1998–1999, Citigroup Peer Set

EMERSON ELECTRIC

This is a firm that built its corporate reputation on the consistency of its earnings. Quarter after quarter it grew its earnings and its corporate reputation. I actually gave speeches about the fact that there were many ways to grow a brand and this was not one of them. I would then explain that Emerson's brand reputation would suffer should they ever miss a quarterly earnings target.

The inevitable happened—the company missed a quarter and got pounded. They finally started running a corporate advertising campaign with the idea that this would fix the problem. Unfortunately, shortsighted, short-term tactical communications are no substitute for managing the corporate brand—as you can see in Figure 20-3.

DAIMLERCHRYSLER

The merger in May 1998 between Daimler-Benz AG and the Chrysler Corporation was supposed to be a "merger of equals." In early 1999,

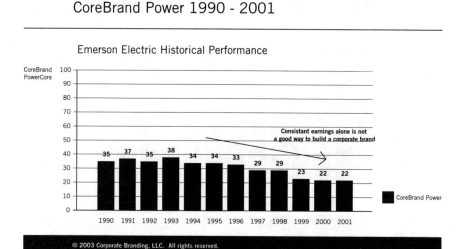

Figure 20-3. CoreBrand Power1990–2001, Emerson Electric Historical Performance

however, DaimlerChrysler CEO Juergen Schrempp told the *Financial Times* that Daimler-Benz had not actually merged with Chrysler, but had acquired it. Schrempp also acknowledged that if Daimler-Benz had made its real intentions known beforehand, it would not have been able to complete the deal.

The name alone was an early indicator that there was something fundamentally wrong with this merger. The illusion of equality ended with the blended corporation's name. It continued into the new company's combined cultures, with the infusion of Daimler management into the top ranks of the Chrysler offices.

Compounding the error, senior management was extremely slow to pick up and correct their mistakes through increased communications, either internally or externally.

In September 2001, *BusinessWeek* wrote, "The merger has so far fallen disastrously short of the goal." As you can see in Figures 20-4 and 20-5, the brand's CoreBrand Power is the lowest among its peers, and its favorability is dropping.

CoreBrand Power 1990 - 2001

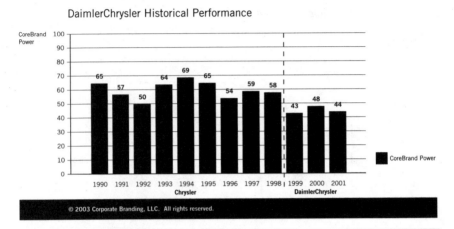

Figure 20-4. CoreBrand Power 1990–2001, DaimlerChrysler Historical
Performance

Familiarity and Favorability 1990 - 2001

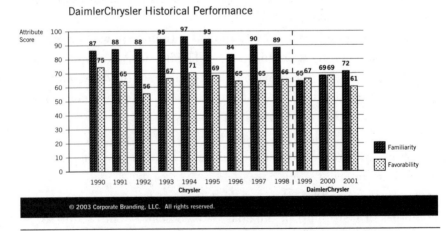

Figure 20-5. Familiarity and Favorability Attributes 1990–2001, Daimler-
Chrysler Historical Performance

Deutsche Bank

Deutsche Bank has been acquiring niche brands for an extended period of time. What it has failed to realize is that those niche brands were known for their specialties: Instead of leveraging those specialties, Deutsche Bank destroyed them by eliminating their brands.

Case in point: Alex Brown was a specialty brokerage firm known in the United States as a company that helped launch initial public offerings (IPOs) for small, growing companies. Deutsche Bank decided to eliminate the name (and the brand image associated with it) in order to have a more cohesive corporate identity. While that sounds logical on the surface, it totally eliminates the value that was created in the first place. Why buy something that you are going to destroy?

Bridgestone/Firestone

When something goes wrong, start pointing fingers.

That's the attitude Bridgestone/Firestone took when its tire treads started separating on Ford Explorers. Flaws in the company's tires, combined with Ford's SUV, are suspected in 88 deaths and 250 injuries on U.S. roads.

Although Bridgestone/Firestone recalled millions of tires, they steadfastly refused to take any responsibility or even acknowledge that there might be design or production flaws in its tires. Instead, the company decided to lay the blame solely with Ford.

In a letter to Ford's then-CEO Jacques Nasser, Bridgestone/Firestone CEO and President John T. Lampe wrote that "Business relationships, like personal ones, are built upon trust and mutual respect . . . We believe they [Ford] are attempting to divert scrutiny of their vehicle by casting doubt on the quality of Firestone tires. The tires are safe, and as we have said before, when we have a problem, we will acknowledge that problem and fix it. We expect Ford to do the same."

Lampe was wrong: The problem was not the trust lost between Ford and Bridgestone/Firestone. The problem was the trust lost between the tire company and its consumers. As the scope of the tragedies

Familiarity 1999 - 4Q 2001

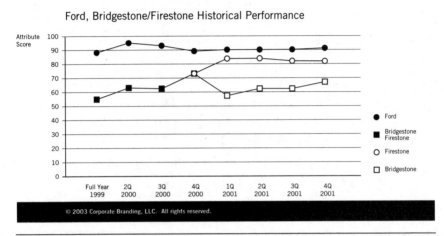

Figure 20-6. Familiarity Attributes 1999–2001, Ford, Bridgestone/Firestone
Historical Performance

Favorability 1999 - 4Q 2001

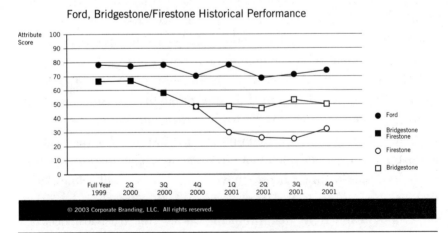

Figure 20-7. Favorability Attributes 1999–2001, Ford, Bridgestone/Firestone
Historical Performance

came to light, the public had two distinct reactions, as shown in Figure 20-6. Familiarity with the Firestone brand climbed sharply, while familiarity with the parent company brand, Bridgestone, temporarily fell away. When Bridgestone/Firestone's corporate reaction became public, the corporate brand again gained familiarity. Unfortunately, this is one of those cases where increased familiarity, for both brands, came for all the wrong reasons. The resulting—and dramatic—decline in favorability is shown in Figure 20-7.

FORD MOTOR COMPANY

Like Bridgestone, Ford was badly damaged by its reaction to the crisis involving its Explorer vehicles and Bridgestone/Firestone tires.

Even before that, however, CEO Jacques Nasser was under fire. In Nasser's 3 years at the helm, Ford experienced increasing problems with quality control, as well as decreasing market share during a more general slump in car and truck sales.

Ford heir William C. Ford replaced Nasser, but not soon enough. Like John T. Lampe, Nasser refused to acknowledge his company's culpability in the deaths and injuries of the people using the Explorer. Nasser also championed the manufacture of increasingly huge SUVs, including the Excursion—a vehicle so massive that it actually ran over cars it hit.

The board should have been more attuned to what was happening when Nasser started destroying brand value and should have acted more decisively to replace him. As shown in Figure 20-6, familiarity with Ford's corporate brand spiked during the tragedies, but soon returned to its previous level. However, as seen in Figure 20-7, its favorability dropped abruptly . . . and long-term favorable perceptions of the company and the brand were put at risk.

Notes

"Bridgestone/Firestone, Inc. Ends Ford Tire Business in the Americas," http://mirror.bridgestone-firestone.com/homeimgs/H010521a. htm.

Lynn Brezosky, "Trial Resumes Monday against Bridgestone/Firestone," Associated Press, http://www.oakridger.com/stories/082001/stt_0820010048.html.

John T. Lampe, Letter to Mr. Jacques Nasser, May 21, 2001, http://www.bridgestone-firestone.com/homeimgs/H010521a.htm.

Dan Neil, "Rumble Seat," http://indyweek.com/durham/2000-05-17/rumble.html.

Richard A. Ryan and Mark Truby, "Firestone, Ford Blame Each Other," *Detroit News*, http://www.detroitnews.com/2000/autos/0009/12/a01-118748.htm.

John S. McClenahen, "Ford and Firestone Separation: Not Just About Tires," industryweek.com, May 30, 2001.

I Index

Note: Page numbers in **bold** indicate display material.